GW00728124

MANAGEMENT

A very comprehensive exposition of the functions of management, as applicable to the various branches of commercial activity — production, selling, financial development and personnel control.

In every way except one, it is a textbook on management; it covers the full scope of the subject; it expounds principles and explains practice; it describes methods and techniques. But it has none of the formality of the textbook . . . We learn our lesson the more readily because the teaching is in our own language of everyday life.

The Times Review of Industry

TEACH YOURSELF BOOKS

MANAGEMENT

M. GILBERT FROST
F.C.C.S., M.I.P.M., A.C.W.A.

TEACH YOURSELF BOOKS
ST. PAUL'S HOUSE WARWICK LANE LONDON EC4

O, that a man might know the end of
this day's business ere it come!
Julius Caesar.

First Printed	1951
Second Edition	1962
Third Edition	1968
This Impression	1972

Third Edition
Copyright © 1968 The English Universities Press Ltd

ISBN 0 340 05646 0

PRINTED AND BOUND IN ENGLAND
FOR THE ENGLISH UNIVERSITIES PRESS LTD
BY HAZELL WATSON AND VINEY LTD, AYLESBURY

CONTENTS

To my God-daughter Angela Thomas,
this edition is dedicated.

FOREWORD

There's no magic in management.

This statement is so important that it deserves a paragraph to itself. Keep it in mind as you read the pages that follow and you will see how true it is.

One of the qualities which a manager must develop is that known as managerial dignity. I shall discuss this in its appropriate place but, for the moment, it will be sufficient for you to realise that it is managerial dignity which, in part, makes the manager's job rather mysterious to those at a lower level. It is my purpose now to look into that mystery and to prove that it hides nothing that plain common sense can't understand and appreciate.

True, considerable study is necessary and something of an aptitude for the work, but, given these, there's no reason why success in the profession of management should not be open to anyone. Remember, there's no magic in management.

London   M. G. F.

In this edition sums of money quoted in sterling are followed, when appropriate, by their decimal equivalents in brackets.

CHAPTER I

How Management has Evolved

The best place to begin the study of any subject is right at the beginning and, for our purpose, I'm going to define this as the period in history when management began to be recognised as something separate from the mechanics of industrial production and commercial enterprise. At the time, that is, when the Family System of manufacture was being superseded by the Domestic System, say about four hundred and fifty years ago.

I'm choosing this period because it marked the beginning of the first recognisable factories though, of course, they were not much like the factories of to-day.

Under the Family System the simple manufactures of the people—mainly weaving and metal work—had been carried out by families in their homesteads. These families combined their handicrafts with, of necessity, their agricultural pursuits. All members of the family worked together, dividing their time, as they saw fit, between tilling the soil and their simple manufactures. They had no power or machinery as we know it to-day.

At about this period the towns began to undergo something of an economic crisis caused, in the main, by what were known as gilds or groups of merchants who had achieved near-monopoly powers and were abusing these powers to the detriment of the more individually-minded merchants who were not gild members. So bad did things become in the towns that these merchants had to seek their livelihood elsewhere. To do this, they went to the villages where the influence of the gilds had not penetrated and where what we should call " private enterprise " was free to develop and reap the rewards appropriate to skill and hard work.

Being men of ability, possessed of intelligence rather above

I

the average, they began to organise the production from their village communities in such a way as to achieve greater output from any given number of workers.

It became the merchants' practice to buy raw materials and to supply them to the workers in their homes. The workers processed them, receiving something in the nature of piece-rate payment for their work, and, in due course, the merchants collected the finished goods and sold them in the most favourable markets they could find. This is what is known as the Domestic System and we see in it the beginnings of the employer-employee relationship which has persisted ever since.

Naturally, there was competition between merchants, each of whom wanted maximum production at minimum cost—there's nothing new in that. Nor is there anything new in the application of astute brains to the problem.

The most obvious solution was to cut the rates of pay to the worker, but this, like so many management problems, wasn't nearly so effective as it might superficially appear to be.

It set up another sort of competition between workers, each of whom tended to break away from the cut-price merchants and offer his services to the better paying ones with the result that, very soon, a minimum wage level came automatically into being.

True, this minimum was a fluctuating one, rising and falling according to the demand for finished products, but, in effect, it caused great distress to many workers and was of little benefit to the merchants who found, as they would if they returned to-day, that if you cut wages below a fair level you will only be able to get the services of the most incompetent workers. They also found, though they may not have appreciated its significance, that a happy and trustful spirit between master and man was one of the most profitable attributes to any business. We shall develop this idea later.

The problem confronting the merchants in the early days of the Domestic System was, then, how to increase output and reduce costs. Wage-cutting had not proved a real solution ; some other must be found.

It was found, again by those of quicker wits, in what we now call specialisation or division of labour—a very important factor in production.

Division of labour means breaking down any production job into constituent parts and giving each part of the work to a specialist worker to perform. Being able to specialise, the worker can become increasingly proficient in his part of the work and can, as a result, work much more quickly and produce better quality. His part of the work done, the part-finished product is passed to the next specialist-worker for further attention.

By passing the raw material through a number of specialists' hands in this way, a greater output of better quality goods can be achieved for any given outgoings in terms of wages.

Just how important a part is played in industry to-day by division of labour can be seen by reference to, say, the printing industry.

So complex are some of the processes in this industry that several years are needed to make a man really proficient in any process. Even then, he still goes on learning and becoming better at his job.

Now, if there were no division of labour, it would mean that all men must be equally good at all printing processes so that each individually would be capable of handling a complete printing job from inception to finished result. Clearly this would be impossible and without division of labour we should be little advanced on Caxton, whose processes were so simple that they could all be carried out by one man.

With division of labour, however, inventive minds have been able to turn their attention to individual processes, to develop them and to devote research to them without having to bother about making them too complicated.

To-day we have specialist compositors, machine minders, lithographers, process-engravers, bookbinders and so on, each of whom has spent many years studying his own process without having to fill his head and his time by mastering the work of other specialists.

I have used the printing industry as an example, but

remember that division of labour has made possible almost the whole of industrial development and it is still going on. More and more complicated processes are being broken down and given to specialists to carry out, every time with added benefit to the consuming public as a whole.

I have dealt with this subject rather extensively because of its importance and I shall return to it again later in its relationship to management. Now, though, we must get back to the Domestic System.

By using a number of cottagers each to perform one process, the merchants found an answer to their demand for increased production at lower cost, but, of course, the idea spread and soon all merchants were employing the same methods so that the same need for cost-reduction arose again at the new level of production. What could be done now?

Mechanise. No longer was hand production fast enough. Mechanical devices had to be invented to speed things up. By this I don't mean complicated machinery such as we know it, but rather what we should call gadgets, hand-operated equipment capable of being installed in the homes of the workers.

The need created the demand for this equipment and the demand found those able and willing to satisfy it.

The next stage, then, was the supplying by the merchants of these mechanical production-aids to the work-people who served them. Unfortunately, these mechanical devices cost money—often more money than the merchant could afford from his capital.

On the other hand, he had to be able to mechanise his source of production or go out of business; he had to borrow money from those better placed financially than he was himself. Here the professional financier comes into the picture.

It is characteristic of financiers that they like to keep an eye on the way their money is being spent and that they like to be as sure as possible that the interest on the loans they make will be paid regularly and that the capital sum will be repaid in due course.

This meant that the merchants who borrowed money to finance the equipping of their cottage-factories were no longer completely free to handle their businesses as they wished. From then on they had to keep one eye on the owner of the money they were using. In his turn, this individual kept both eyes on the way his money was being spent.

No longer could the merchant reward his workers as he alone thought fit, no longer could he fix his own prices, no longer could he choose his own markets. All these considerations were now subject to the permission of the financier as a condition for the loan of the money.

I am quite sure that the discerning reader will, at this point, have noticed something that the merchant of the Domestic System probably never considered at all. His status was changing, slowly and, to him, imperceptibly but, nevertheless, changing.

Before the coming of the financier on to the scene, the merchant had been master of all his activities, completely free to conduct his business as he wished. Working under the eye of the financier he had become something of a middleman between the financier on one side and the workers on the other.

In short, his job now was to direct the human activities of his workers in such a way as to satisfy the legitimate demands of the financier and himself draw a reward in proportion to the success of his efforts. He had become a manager.

This would probably be a good place at which to end the chapter but something more remains to be explained if we are to have a clear understanding of the link between the Domestic System Manager and the Factory System Manager of to-day.

It was, among other things, the application of steam power to machinery that translated the Domestic into the Factory System.

For centuries, industrial production had plodded forward almost without noticeable change in method from generation to generation until, with startling suddenness, the whole social, economic and industrial life of the country turned a somersault—or at least, an industrial revolution.

In the main, this was because of the inescapable physical requirement that a power-driven machine should be attached to a power source and there could only be a limited number of power sources.

The immediate effect of this was to denude the workers' cottages of machinery, to force on workers the need to attend full-time at a factory or full-time in agriculture and to give rise to factories of all sorts near the coal-bearing areas of the country.

A secondary effect of some significance was the need for workers to abandon their handicraft skills and become servants of machines—a very different kind of skill.

From the point of view of management, however, the most important effect of the application of steam power to machinery is related to capital expense.

The capital required to set up a factory was obviously greater than could be loaned by any one financier and groups of persons with money combined to finance factories on a joint basis—a basis which eventually gave rise to the joint stock company of to-day.

Thus the technical man in charge of the factory, the counterpart of the practical merchant of the Domestic System, was responsible to a financial body comprising a number of people. These bodies were even more difficult of access and less accommodating than the individual financier had been.

To add to his trouble, the man in charge of the factory had a much larger number of work-people to handle than had his Domestic System precursor.

On top of all this, his workers, who had hoped for a golden age, were now being disillusioned rapidly, grievances were rife, trouble-makers were ready for action and there was no end to the demands for better conditions, more pay, shorter hours and other amenities.

As these demands could only be met with the consent of the financial sponsors who had little or no interest in anything but the return on their money, the poor factory manager, as we now recognise him, was in a very unpleasant position. He had to keep his workers working and satisfy the owners' requirements in the matter of profits.

It is to their credit that many of these managers did a splendid job of work within the limitations set them by circumstances, but their lot was not an enviable one and the conditions under which they worked could not be perpetuated indefinitely.

It would be interesting to go more fully into the growth and composition of the opposing forces, the trade unions on the one hand, combinations and monopolies on the other, but to do so would be to digress from our subject. Remember only that at this period in history began that artificial hostility between capital and labour interests that has persisted ever since. I have said " artificial " and shall hope, in due course, to prove the fitness of this adjective.

It would be interesting, too, to follow the effect of the Industrial Revolution on the transport systems of the country, the improvement in road-making, the increase in canal transport and its decrease with the coming of the railways. This, too, would be a digression but the reader is recommended to study these things elsewhere if he wants to combine a really interesting pursuit with a useful background knowledge of industry.

It is our job, in this book, to consider the manager who, during the years of the Industrial Revolution, was in a most difficult and virtually untenable position between financial interests and workers. His position in the industrial scene had to be clarified and his job given a proper status.

A great deal of thought was given to this problem, but it was not until the close of the nineteenth century that any real attempt was made to recognise that there is a substantial scientific element in management, to see just what management was and what its practice required. Only after that had been done could principles be evolved, courses of study established and research devoted to the many outstanding problems that remained—and still remain—to be solved.

CHAPTER II

What Management Is

There have been many attempts to define management, some good, some too detailed for easy understanding, some wide of the mark, but for our purpose in this chapter I am going to define management as the art and science of directing human activities. Remember that—the art and science of directing human activities.

Now let's turn to the popular conception of management and see just where it's wrong.

Because management is the art and science of directing human activities, it follows that to be a director of a company is not, of itself, to be a manager. True, a director may be the head of a department, in which latter capacity he directs the activities of others and, by definition, manages. In the Board Room, however, he directs the company, not the activities of others.

It also follows that technical activities are not management. Technical decisions are often made by managers but, in making these decisions, they are not acting as managers.

I have a feeling that the last two paragraphs, though stating simple truths in simple words, may yet have left the reader somewhat confused. This, if true, is not the reader's fault, nor, I hope, is it mine. Let's examine the subject in rather more detail.

Consider in your mind's eye any industrial company, large or small, with which you have a nodding acquaintance. You will be aware that it consists of three main groups of people; first the directors, secondly the group comprising those known as managers and supervisors, including heads of departments, foremen and the like and, thirdly, the group generally known as the operatives and office staff who carry out the manual and clerical tasks in the factory and office.

There are, of course, many other groupings that could be devised but, for our purpose, this simple arrangement will suffice.

I want you to forget for the moment that single individuals may, especially in a small company, be members of all three groups. Forget that a director may be head of a department and also act as a salesman on occasion. This often happens, but to keep thinking of it confuses the explanation. Once the true concept of management is appreciated, these confusing factors can be dealt with quite easily. We assume, then, that each of the three groups consists of individuals who have no place in either of the other two.

Remembering always that management consists of directing the activities of others, look first at the Board of Directors. What does it do ? And how does it do it ?

Without attempting to list its duties and methods in any order of importance, it can be said that the Board's responsibility is to define the policy of the company and thereby to provide an objective and a reason for the company's existence. The policy established will cover such matters as what to make, how much to make, where and when to make it, how much to sell it for and many other details which, taken together, comprise a broad plan of action to be carried out during some fixed future period.

Another task of the Board is to satisfy itself that the policy previously laid down is being observed and to examine any variation from it.

Having satisfied itself that policy is being followed and that it will continue to be followed, the Board may advise as to how it shall be implemented by the managing director ; they may, alternatively, leave all the detail to him.

There are, too, many legal requirements to which a company must conform and the Board, with the advice of its Secretary, will see that the law is being observed.

Finally, though possibly not exhaustively, the Board will authorise expenditure of a capital nature, sanction plans for major expansion or contraction projects and keep itself informed on all financial matters relevant to company prosperity.

If it were possible to condense even this short list into one sentence, it would be broadly true to say that the Board is the watch-dog of the shareholders whose interests it represents and who, of course, elect it for just that purpose.

I hope that some among my readers will have noted that not one of these responsibilities of the Board involves any direction of the activities of others. It is the company's affairs the Board is directing; not the activities of those whom the company employs. It follows that directors do not manage and that any study of management need concern itself very little with a director's work and responsibility.

Now to the next group—that containing those known as managers, heads of departments, supervisors, foremen and so on—to what extent do these people direct the activities of others ?

At once we can see that they have quite a lot to do with the direction of the activities of others, and this applies not only to those styled as managers, overseers and the like ; it applies all down the line from senior to junior excluding only the very few at the bottom who have no one below them whose activities to direct.

At this point, then, the original three groups—Directors, Managers and operatives—have merged into two since we have already dismissed Directors; we can also dismiss those of the operatives who carry so little responsibility that they do not control the activities of anyone but themselves.

This leaves us with a group of people all of whom perform a certain amount of management in their work. It will pay us to examine this group in some detail.

It consists of everyone in any organisation except those whose duties are solely directorial; it includes the managing director, his subordinate executives, their staffs, the foremen, chargehands, section-hands and those who have no responsibility for any actions other than their own. These last are surprisingly few in number and can, by definition, be eliminated on the same grounds as those on which we eliminated the directors—they do not include management in their duties because these are purely technical, using this term to include office work as well as the more generally accepted mechanical processes.

Turning now to the remainder, we can see that, with one exception, the duties of each one of them include a proportion of technical and a proportion of managerial responsibility. The exception is the managing director who, for present purposes, can be assumed to be solely responsible for management, having no technical side to his work at all.

Of the rest, it is clear that the proportion of management to technical responsibilities varies in accordance with the status of the individual in the undertaking.

At the lower end of the scale, there is the chargehand, or section-hand, who is himself an operative with a machine to tend or other manual work to do. This takes up most of his time but, nevertheless, he has a number of subordinates whose activities he has to direct.

At a higher level, the foreman has many technical pursuits, including work-instruction, decisions of a technical nature and, possibly, some mechanical duties to perform. He, though, has many more people under him, including the chargehands, whose activities he has to direct.

What of the works manager, probably a senior executive of the company ? Obviously, he must have quite a fund of technical knowledge and some of his time is spent in using that knowledge in the interests of the company, but the major proportion of his time will be spent in directing the activities of his numerous subordinates.

To sum up so far, then, every business organisation contains a large group of people all concerned in some degree with management and all practising management. With the exception of the managing director, the responsibilities of each one of the group combine managerial and technical duties. At the bottom, these responsibilities are predominantly technical ; at the top, predominantly managerial.

Further, as each member of the group achieves promotion, so does the managerial side of his job occupy an increasingly greater proportion of his time at the expense of the technical. By the time he becomes managing director, there are, anyway in a large organisation, so few technical demands made on him that his job can be said to be purely managerial.

If this is not clear, it is very important indeed that this chapter should be read and re-read to this point until it is clear, since all that follows is linked to the modern concept of management just explained.

Having come to a sound understanding of what is involved in management, we can now forget all about the various groups of people and deal only with one group—those who, in varying degrees, exercise managerial responsibility from the junior chargehand and the next-to-last office junior at the bottom to the managing director at the top ; no doubt this group will include almost all those who read this book.

It will now be helpful if the reader will carefully consider his own job in relation to what he has read and ask himself how much of it is management, how much of it technical or, we can now say, clerical ? It may be said that the two aspects of his job do exist but that they are so inextricably mixed up that it is impossible to sort them out. In case someone does feel this way, let me put the question another way. How many of the problems of the job spring from (a) technical origins and how many from (b) the subordinates for whose activities he is responsible ? Would it be very wrong to say that, at office manager level anyway, nearly all the problems are of the latter category ? A well-trained individual with experience is unlikely to have many headaches of a technical or clerical origin ; if so, then, unless his job never presents any problems—an impossible hypothesis—it follows that his problems mainly arise from his responsibility for his subordinates' activities ; in short, they are managerial problems.

Now this is rather more than an academic argument for, at least, two reasons.

First, it means that management can be studied, practised and applied as a science in its own right.

Secondly, it is not possible any longer to say with conviction that management of an engineering firm is distinct from management of, say, a printing firm, an hotel or a firm of solicitors. In every case there are subordinates with activities to be directed and the argument developed in preceding pages holds good.

It is on these two postulates that all management training is based.

Of course, directing the activities of subordinates is a substantial task and calls for something more than a sense of discipline. Were this not so, any competent school-master or Service officer would be, automatically, a good manager and we cannot presume that this is necessarily true.

To avoid confusion in this way, therefore, I am going to expand our definition of management without in any way cutting across what has already been discussed. I am going to say that management is the art of directing human activities in such a way as to achieve the greatest possible measure of conformity with company policy. Read that again.

It follows, then, that the good manager must not only know how to handle his subordinates and how to guide their efforts ; he must also know where to guide them. Discipline alone without a sense of direction is not good business management.

It is this fact which makes a book like this necessary, since the acquisition of a sense of direction can only follow a full understanding of the many factors which impinge on policy. In other words, the good manager must be able to understand the whys and wherefores of policy before he can attempt to direct his subordinates in conformity with it. In subsequent chapters we shall deal with these manifold matters but first I must say a few words on organisation since this pervades all a manager's actions.

The more senior a manager is, the more of his time is devoted to management—we have already discussed this. Clearly, then, the more senior he is, the greater in number are his individual responsibilities. To see this clearly, think again of the junior employee with one man's activities to supervise and the managing director who has to concern himself with full responsibility for the conduct of the business in all its aspects—selling, producing, finance, development and that host of difficulties classed as human element problems. Are we to take it, then, that to be a good manager a man must be expert in all these things ? The answer is no ; there's no magic in management.

What the good manager must do, however, is group his responsibilities under the headings listed—they are known as functions of management—and put one or more groups under the care of individual executives ranking next in line to himself, thereby creating a team of experts of which the managing director is, as it were, the captain.

Each of his senior executives—or team members—will, by this means, be able to specialise in one or more of the functions entrusted to him—selling, producing, finance, development and personnel relations—and will become a specialist adviser to the managing director.

In this way the managing director will have only to deal with five or six specialists instead of having to pass his instructions out to innumerable subordinates in numerous departments. By dealing in this way with a few experts only, and by giving and receiving all information through their agency, the managing director is observing what is known as the span of control—a dictum which states that no man, however able, can efficiently and capably deal directly with more than five or six subordinates for whose activities he is immediately responsible. Many would-be managers fail lamentably to recognise the truth of this.

The picture I want you to have in mind now, then, is that of the managing director as the active captain of a team, each member of which is a specialist in one or other of the functions of management. It is for the managing director to interpret policy into terms applicable to each of his specialists and to instruct them accordingly.

Having been broadly instructed as to what is required of them, the specialists will carry out in detail, through their own subordinates, the execution of the instructions and will report back to the managing director.

He will then collate the information into such form as will indicate the progress made and will report back to the Board accordingly.

In order to do this intelligently, it is not necessary for the managing director to be himself a specialist in each of the functions, but he must, obviously, know the capabilities of each, what it embraces, how it can be used and how actual performance can be judged against optimum performance. A good analogy is that of an organist. He need not know how his instrument is made in order to get the very best out of it by knowing exactly what stop to bring in and cut out at any given moment. He must know what effect to expect from the use of each of his stops but he need not have detailed knowledge of how they work. So a good managing director knows exactly how and when to use each of his subordinates, he knows what to ask of them and what to expect—but he need not know, in detail, how each one achieves the results he desires.

To sum up, a good manager needs to be able to interpret policy into terms of the functions of management and to be able to use those functions as tools in the conversion of policy into fact.

The remaining chapters will be devoted to providing the necessary background knowledge to interpret policy and the necessary knowledge of the functions to make possible their use as tools of management.

CHAPTER III

The Manager as Economist

I would like to be able to say that, in this chapter, I propose to deal with all the economic problems likely to confront any manager. Unfortunately, I cannot say this nor, judging by the many large volumes written on the subject by others, can anyone else claim to have dealt with them exhaustively.

I have tried here to outline the major points which a manager will need to understand when interpreting instructions passed to him and when giving instructions to his own subordinates. There are, though, certain economic laws and principles which are not subject to divergences of opinion and it is these which I have tried to present for the guidance of the manager.

Economic thinking is necessary in this context because the success of a manager depends on his ability to direct the activities of others in conformity with company policy; it is logical to expect a manager to be able to interpret policy and to know the reasons underlying the demands that his Board of Directors makes on him.

As far as the managing director is concerned, of course, he will have a seat on the Board and will take his share in framing policy—but not all managers are managing directors. Heads of departments, foremen, chargehands and all others with any managerial responsibilities will be in the less fortunate position of having policy dictated to them with little or no say in its framing. Their job is to carry it out.

To do this adequately requires that they shall be provided with clear instructions and explanations—very important this—from the managing director. Given these, their success or failure as managers must rest on their own managerial ability.

We see, then, that management, as we have defined it,

needs an intelligent appreciation of the underlying reasons for policy and an ability accurately to predict the effects of any action taken to implement that policy. A manager, in short, must be something of an economist.

By this I don't mean that he need necessarily have made a deep study of economics—though such a study would be an invaluable attribute—but he must know enough elementary economics to guide him in understanding the purport of his instructions, in his methods of executing them, and in solving some of the many managerial problems that will come his way.

Perhaps the first question, on the answer to which the manager must be absolutely clear, is this. Why is my company in business at all ?

Discount at once the first answer that comes to mind— that the company exists to make money—and think more deeply.

Is it true that the only satisfaction to be derived from being in business is to make money ? I think not. Of course profits must be made, or, at least, the income of any business must, over a period, be sufficient to pay the outgoings and provide for conservation of the assets and, of course, business success is measured in money units because these can be universally understood. But is money the whole reason ?

If it were, surely the most happy and respected person would be the business man who had succeeded in cutting wages, economising on factory amenities and forcing up prices in all cases to a greater extent than his competitors ? Is this so ?

No, there are many more high principled reasons for being in business and these reasons will play their part from time to time, and often subconsciously, in the minds of the directors.

There is a lot of gratification to be had from the knowledge that, through one's efforts, some human want is being satisfied ; that one's employees are being given good jobs, are being cared for and looked after ; that, in however small a way, one's country is being assisted in its overseas trade.

There is also the sporting instinct that finds pleasure in meeting problems, analysing them, and solving them. There is the comradeship that comes from contact with well-trusted colleagues; the spirit that inspires a team.

These are some of the reasons that keep people in business and they apply, you will see, to some extent to all those with a managerial side to their jobs. It may be that you can think of many other reasons but the point to remember is that money alone is not the sole driving force that keeps a manager at his desk.

A prosperous managing director recently expressed the opinion, in conversation, that the only reason he stayed in business was to become as rich as he could. He probably thought he really meant this until someone suggested that if he sold all his interests and invested the proceeds, he could nearly double his income. Why, he was asked, didn't he retire and do this if all he wanted was material wealth?

Being a fair-minded man, he admitted at once that he had spoken hastily and joined in the ensuing discussion on the question I have posed here. Since then I have asked the same question—why are you in business?—of many other successful men and I have never met one who would prefer a life of idle riches to taking the risks and knocks of business life.

Remember, then, when following instructions from the Board, that money-making, whether the directors know it or not, is not their only object.

Leaving this aspect of economics, I pass on now to another which I have already dealt with in some detail in Chapter I—division of labour. It is so important that I am going to discuss it again here.

You will remember that, in essence, division of labour implies the breaking down of complex operations into small and more simple ones which can more easily and quickly be learnt by the worker of average intelligence.

Of course, the extent to which labour is divided depends

substantially not only on the industry being considered but also on the precise factory within that industry.

Thus, to take clothing, there will be the large clothing factories where suits are cut out scores at a time to standard patterns, and there will be the working tailor making up suits to fit individual customers.

In the former case, division of labour will play a big part since the output of suits will be considerable and it would be impossible to employ highly skilled cutters for each garment without putting the price of the finished suit outside the range of the lower-income groups. To do this would so restrict demand that the factory could not operate at an economic level.

In the latter case, the working tailor does not want to get orders for hundreds of suits, he wants only sufficient orders to keep him busy ; further, his overhead expenses are low and a week or two of slack trade will not seriously trouble him. He, therefore, need indulge in very little division of labour ; rather will he prefer to give personal attention to all details so as to keep a wealthy clientele who can afford to pay high prices for hand-tailored suits.

With these two extremes before it, any Board of Directors is confronted with the problem of how much division of labour to apply to its own business. Is it better to break down processes, employ less skilled labour and mechanise to the maximum with the object of capturing a wide market for cheap—though not necessarily inferior—goods ? Or is it better to retain individual craftsmen and limited mechanisation and sell the product in the more expensive range ? Somewhere between these extremes lies the right answer on which to base policy.

The Board concerned will, if it be wise, undertake research into the available markets at several previously calculated price levels : it will bear in mind the maximum and minimum economic capacities of its plant and it will consider the extent to which its processes can be broken down if necessary. With this information, the decision must be taken.

This, however, applies mainly to those firms who are in a

position to decide in advance the production schedule. It applies, for example, to manufacturers of household goods, bicycles and all that host of items which are manufactured before being sold to the consumer through the retail market. What, then, is the position of the man who manufactures to the individual customer's order—the printer, the small tailor and the picture-framer, for instance ? What part, if any, does division of labour play in the economies of their businesses ?

In case the distinction between these two categories of manufacturers is not quite clear, it will be helpful to distinguish them in rather more detail in the process of answering these questions.

In all firms someone has to initiate production, as it is called, or, in more homely terms, start the wheels turning. Now in the former category of manufacturers, it is the Board of Directors which decides how much to make and what to charge for it. The Board then starts the wheels turning by authorising production to begin. It is the sales manager's task to sell the output after it is in existence.

In the latter category of firms, usually small but far more numerous than many people imagine, the wheels cannot start turning until a customer has appeared in the office and placed a specific order and only a continuity of such orders can keep the firm running economically. In this case, then, it is the sales manager who has to get the orders in advance of production and it is he who initiates production. You will see that the emphasis is completely different in the two categories. Be clear on this because we shall refer to it again later on. For the moment, though, we are considering what part division of labour can play in the life of the small—or job-production—manufacturer.

The job-production man obviously cannot break down his processes and employ specialist personnel to any great extent because he never knows from one day to the next what processes will be required in connection with orders received : nor would specialist personnel be a lot of good when constantly varying demands are being made on his productive resources.

This, though, doesn't mean that he can ignore the economics and efficiencies inherent in the principle of division of labour but it does mean that he must secure its advantages in another way. He must, as a firm, specialise.

The temptation ever present to inveigle the job-producer is the inclination to take any order offered provided it can conceivably be handled in his factory. In this he is wrong and will sooner or later find himself saddled with hosts of orders which he can only satisfy by turning his plant upside down and producing completely uneconomically.

His policy, then, must be one of specialisation. He should consider carefully the type or types of goods which he is best equipped to manufacture. Of these, he should consider the type or types of goods which he can manufacture most profitably. He should then specialise in the production of these types of goods to the exclusion, as far as possible, of all others, the orders for which will eventually find their way to manufacturers specialising in them.

In this way the job-production manufacturer can avail himself of the benefits of division of labour, since he is, in fact, applying the principle on a plant basis instead of an operative basis. Instead of employing specialist personnel, he is thinking in terms of specialist plant.

In all this chapter so far, little mention has been made of prices—a very important consideration to any manufacturer or commercial concern. To what extent, then, are prices subject to economic regulation ? Again, the answer is one not generally realised by those members of the public who have not had managerial experience.

Ask most people what fixes prices and they will say that prices are fixed by costs. They will explain that a costing system is used to determine the total cost of a product, that a profit margin is then added and the resulting figure is the price. This is not so ; costs are fixed by prices.

At first glance this may seem rather a stupid remark, but it is true, as you will see if we look into it a bit further.

If you look around the shops in your neighbourhood you will find that there is a narrow price range for each kind of goods, irrespective of the manufacturer. Electric irons, for example, are made by many firms but you will find that electric irons that are similar in utility are similar in price. If one is much cheaper than the others it is because it is fitted with fewer refinements or is of a less attractive finish.

It is possible to deduce from this, then, that there is some factor tending to equalise prices for similar articles.

Now suppose that one manufacturer puts an electric iron on the market at twice the price of his nearest competitor. Unless that iron be twice as good—and we will assume that it is not—he won't sell any until he has reduced his price to approximately his competitor's level.

Again, let us suppose that a manufacturer markets an electric iron at half the price of that sold by his nearest competitor. It can only be sold at such a price by ignoring the cost of production. The manufacturer will sell many thousands but since he will be losing money on each one he sells, every sale will increase the speed with which he goes out of business unless he raises his price to approximately that of his competitors and we are back again where we started with all comparable irons at comparable prices.

To develop the argument still further we must go behind the scenes to the Board Room of an electric iron manufacturer where price policy is being discussed.

On the table will be all available details of quality offered and prices charged by competitors and the decision the Board will have to take is this. Are we going to produce a better iron than our competitors and thus justify entry into the top end of the price range, being content to sell comparatively few as a result ? Or are we going to produce a mass-production job in large quantities as cheaply as possible and break into the lower end of the price range ?

To help them in this decision the directors will have instructed the managing director to obtain, through the sales manager, market surveys. We shall talk of these later but for the moment it will be sufficient to explain that a market survey indicates roughly how many irons can be sold at different price levels.

With this information before it, the Board will decide, let's say, to go for the quantity market at low prices. It will set that price just below that of its nearest competitor and will instruct the managing director to streamline the production organisation until the quantity produced and total production cost per iron (which normally falls as output rises) make it possible to sell economically at the price decided on in the Board Room.

Remember, then, that every item has an economic price range above which it cannot be sold and below which it can only be sold at a loss. It is the object of good management to reduce the cost per unit to such an extent that a profit can be made by selling within the economic price range. Costs, therefore, are fixed by prices.

Discussion of prices brings inevitably to mind the retail shop and, by inference, the retailer and wholesaler. What is their place in the economic structure of business management ?

There are those who incline to the view that any person or organisation intervening between the manufacturer and the consumer must, if a profit be taken, be something of a parasite.

If, say these people, a factory in Yorkshire can make an article profitably for ten shillings and if it costs two shillings to transport that article to the consumer, anything over twelve shillings of the price paid in a shop is an imposition for the purpose of supporting and providing for the middleman. On the face of it, this seems an arguable case. Like so many things that seem crystal clear at first glance, however, this argument, except in a very few isolated cases, collapses in face of the more detailed thinking which we must now devote to it. For a change, we'll draw our conclusions in terms of door-knobs.

Let us suppose that there are six factories, all making door-knobs, dotted about the country and let us suppose that there are countless builders and private householders all in need of door-knobs. Let us suppose, too, that there are no wholesalers or retailers trading in the door-knob market.

The first problem to be solved would be the means whereby door-knob makers and door-knob needers could be put in touch with each other. Advertising on a grand scale might possibly help but it would hardly be an adequate solution. Mrs. H. of Finsbury Park might be a door-knob needer but it might well be that her reading matter did not include any advertisements by door-knob makers. Even if it did contain advertisements of one or two makers, Mrs. H. would not have much of a selection to choose from.

Let us assume, then, that all door-knob makers advertised in all papers in such a way that every potential door-knob needer could not help seeing advertisements from all the door-knob makers. This is an impossible theory and would, if practicable, be so costly that the price of door-knobs would be prohibitive. However, for the sake of argument, let's suppose this actually happens.

Mrs. H. would then certainly be able to see what each manufacturer thinks about his own door-knobs, she would know his prices and his address. She would then have to select the one she thought most suited to her needs, sit down and write a letter, make out a cheque or get a postal order and send off her money into the blue hoping that, when the door-knob arrived, it would really be what she wanted. If it weren't, of course, endless correspondence would have to pass between her and the manufacturer before, if ever, she got satisfaction.

Look now at what all this would mean at the manufacturer's end. He would need an army of clerks, a regiment of book-keepers, a huge packing and dispatch department and an immense building to house all these. He might, too, need flocks of commercial travellers to back up his press advertising campaign. In short, his overhead expenses would be such as to put door-knobs in the same price range as fine jewellery—that is, outside the economic price range of door-knobs.

Having argued the matter to the point of absurdity, we

can now see much more clearly what the wholesaler and retailer really do for the livings they earn.

First, they make possible the bulk ordering and delivery of products, thereby simplifying immensely the manufacturers' troubles. Secondly, they make available to the purchaser a full selection of all the goods available so that they can be examined and bought with certainty that they will be suitable.

Thirdly, by handling themselves the myriad small cash transactions and paying the manufacturer in lump-sums, they simplify his accounting systems. Fourthly, in the performance of these services, they make it possible for the manufacturer so to reduce his costs that he can sell at a price within the economic price range—even though the wholesaler's and retailer's profits have to be found in the final price to the consumer.

I have, for my purpose, considered wholesaler and retailer as identical. In fact, of course, they both perform the same service at different stages on the route of the product to the consumer and, by thinking along the lines indicated, the reader will have no difficulty in putting each in his proper perspective.

Another factor, still with a relationship to prices, which will cause earnest concern to the directors establishing policy in a new firm is this. How large—or small—shall the firm be ?

Clearly, no set of standard rules can be laid down since the answer all depends on factors individual to each case. Some generalisations, though, will be worth considering.

A wise Board will realise that there is an optimum size for every firm relative to the work intended to be carried out. For example, a firm whose market surveys showed a potential market capacity of a hundred thousand units of output per annum would be unwise to plan a factory capable of turning out substantially more than this quantity. On the other hand, a firm with a believed market capacity virtually unlimited would be wise to set an initial output target and construct the factory with this in mind, taking all possible steps to permit of expansion at need while refraining from committing itself to such expansion in advance.

Secondly, the Board faced with the problem of size will remember that cost per unit tends to drop as output increases—why this happens will be explained elsewhere. To complicate matters, however, this is only true up to a point and it may well be that cost per unit may begin to rise once a certain level of output has been reached. Such a phenomenon might occur, for example, when a factory is producing to capacity with cost per unit at its lowest. To produce more, new buildings must be acquired and new plant bought; new executive personnel may be required and the result of all this may be that the cost per unit over all may rise as additional output is produced. Once it has risen, of course, the decline will set in again until the capacity of the new plant is fully absorbed, when the same sequence of events will happen again.

Bear in mind, then, when interpreting what may seem a strange policy decision that there is an optimum size for every undertaking and the wise Board is constantly seeking either to find that size for the current output or to adjust that output up or down so as to bring the existing size of the business into conformity with the optimum output.

Sometimes these efforts to achieve optimum size and maximum efficiency result in various forms of amalgamation, merger and combine. These take many shapes and are, in the main, aimed at the elimination of competition.

The Board may think it wise to buy up a competitor and extinguish him that way; it may prefer to enter into some agreement with a competitor such that each firm can specialise as explained earlier. In this case, unsuitable orders offered to one firm would be transferred to the other to carry out.

Again, by agreement, firms can arrange to allocate sales areas, each operating without competition in clearly defined parts of the country or of the world. Immense savings in sales expenses can be achieved in this way.

Or a Board may find that the cost of its raw materials is such that it would be more advantageous to acquire financial control of its supply houses and thus share in the profit accruing from its own extensive dealings with them. If it then takes over its suppliers in this way, a start is made in the formation of a vertical combine or combination of firms, each of whom is the consumer of the other's products. Such a combine might embrace, for instance, a pulp importer, a paper maker, a printer, a bookbinder and a bookseller.

Finally, under this heading, there is the horizontal combine. Here, a number of firms in the same line of business unite together under one controlling interest. All orders received can then be channelled to the factory best equipped to handle them. It is also possible to close down uneconomic factories and to re-equip the remainder to enable them to specialise for the common good of all.

Even though this chapter is tending to become somewhat lengthy, I must find space to include one more consideration likely to concern the Board of a new firm. Where shall it be ?

It can be near its raw materials, near its market or distant from both. The deciding factors are simple and can be dealt with quite briefly.

The first practical factor to be weighed is that of the relative bulk and transportability of the raw materials, including fuel, and those of the finished goods. Easily transported light-weight products requiring substantial quantities of heavy mineral substances for their manufacture would obviously be more economically made in a district near where the raw materials originate, whereas the reverse would apply to bulky, awkward, perishable or fragile finished goods likely to be expensive to transport to their market.

Some processes again—paper making is one—require a continuous flow of water and are thus forced to select sites near rivers or canals.

Further, all factories need labour and it would be useless to set up a plant in an area where labour was not available or where housing was deficient.

Another factor determining location of any factory is that of waste-disposal. Some processes give rise to by-products of a saleable nature; where this is the case, it may be worth considering whether to set up the plant in the neighbourhood of competitors in the same line of business with a view to increasing the likelihood of selling the waste and tapping a supply of trained labour.

Such are the main considerations to be considered when deciding where to set up a factory, though there are other, perhaps more obvious, ones that will come to mind without prompting. They include the cost of land, possibility of expansion, charges for electricity and gas, rateable value of property and consideration of local by-laws which, in some districts, may effectively prohibit the establishment of a factory altogether. These, however, can only be usefully discussed in relation to specific plans.

CHAPTER IV

The Manager as Psychologist

To attempt to deal comprehensively with the subject of psychology in one chapter would be to attempt the impossible. Psychology is a science of almost infinite complexity on which it is probable that there will always be much conflict of opinion.

It is, nevertheless, essential that the practising manager shall have a working knowledge of the subject if he is to do his job adequately.

If support be needed for this contention, it is to be found in the definition that management is the art and science of directing human activities. It follows that the more one knows about human activities and their motives, the more successfully will one be able to direct them in conformity with company policy. Let this simple truth be our text for this chapter.

Now it is clearly of the greatest importance that every employee should be as happy as possible in his work and, to achieve this, that the work given to any employee should be well matched to his ability.

Nothing is more soul-destroying to the intelligent man than to have to fill in his working day performing a task that could well be performed by a child ; nothing is more harassing than to be given work calling for greater skill and experience than he possesses.

(Incidentally, to simplify reading, I am using the masculine gender though my remarks apply equally to the feminine.)

In all too many cases, when a vacancy occurs in any business, it is filled in the most casual way. A few applicants are seen and the first one showing any intelligence is selected to fill the vacancy, the general idea being that job and man will jointly rub the edges off each other until something of a fit is obtained. A really contented staff cannot be recruited by these methods

—and the wise manager brings much more thought to the problem.

We shall be dealing with job analysis and job specification later in the book and it would only confuse the issue to try and explain here what they are. Take it on trust then, that they are among the means used to assess the qualities or aptitudes required for the satisfactory performance of any job, technical or clerical, in the organisation. Only by assessing the sort of man wanted for a job can any real attempt be made to find a man likely to be happy in it.

This brings us to the subject of aptitude tests. These are serious attempts to assess, in advance, the technical and manipulative ability possessed by an applicant in relation to a specific task which it is intended that he shall perform if appointed.

In order to set an aptitude test, it is essential that the manager shall have had the task carefully analysed with expert skill in order to determine the aptitudes required to perform it. On the basis of this analysis, the test is set.

Aptitude tests are open to many abuses. To avoid these, the tests should be set and their results measured by a trained man with long experience. Even so, they are a means only of testing an aptitude; they are not substitutes for an interview.

Some jobs, for example, call for an ability to spend many hours on boring routine work, others for a mechanical ability, a mathematical ability or for an interest in experimental work, and there are many other abilities called for in varying proportions by varying jobs.

Obviously, it is unlikely that one will find, at need, an applicant possessing in the right proportion all the abilities required by the vacancy to be filled; the next best thing is to find an applicant who has the right aptitudes and to convert these into the specialised abilities by training.

For this reason, an aptitude test does not often bear any apparent relationship to the actual technical or clerical job to which it is directed. There's no need for it to, really, as only the aptitude of the individual is being tested, not his practical ability.

Aptitude tests may include dismantling and re-assembling some simple mechanical device, the insertion of pegs in a moving perforated band, tests for colour sense, or they may be paper and pencil tests in which the applicant is asked to answer certain questions framed in a particular way or to indicate on a diagram which of a selection of alternative designs he would use to complete a given pattern. As already explained, however, there are as many aptitude tests as there are jobs to be tested and the warning must be repeated.

Get a book on aptitude testing by all means—you'll find it absorbingly interesting—but don't attempt to apply the tests to actual cases without, at least, the advice of someone who has had great experience of their uses, advantages and weaknesses.

I mustn't let it be thought that, given a properly set aptitude test, the need for personal interview with the applicant is unnecessary. Far from it.

As has been said, an aptitude test is not a substitute for an interview at which many other characteristics will become apparent to the trained interviewer. An aptitude test cannot assess personality or that nebulous thing called character; these are equally important qualities in deciding which applicant to appoint to a specific job, working under a known foreman or chargehand—who also has personal idiosyncrasies of his own which must be taken into account when interviewing potential staff for him.

In the factory or office of to-day there is little room for the bad-mixer, the misanthrope or the lone-wolf. True, there are a few jobs that can be given to these types but, in the main, the best employee is one who can fit comfortably into the working group and this particular quality can only be really tested at interview. An aptitude test must, therefore, be supported by a personal interview.

The interviewer can be the personnel manager, if there be one, or the head of the department in which the newcomer is destined to work ; in either case this latter should certainly have the final voice in any decision to engage.

Since so much depends on the results of the interview, it is only logical to require that the interviewer shall know something about interviewing. It is surprising, in fact, how few people can conduct a fruitful interview.

Most interviewing technique comes from practice and experience but there are some useful hints that can be mastered and committed to mind as a foundation on which to base experience as it is acquired.

Remember first, then, that absolute sincerity is necessary in the interviewer. He must never give the impression that he is hiding something or keeping something back from the candidate. Only a sincerely frank and open approach to the candidate can elicit the same in return.

Next, the interviewer must never lose sight of the fact that the candidate is probably nervous or anxious and he may well be one of those who cannot make the best of themselves under trying conditions. The interviewer, then, will spend some time and great patience in putting the candidate at his ease and in making allowances for his mental state. Time and thought devoted to this are never wasted.

Having got the candidate into a more relaxed state, the interviewer can proceed either on guided or unguided lines, the choice depending substantially on the type of job for which the candidate is being interviewed and on the experience of the interviewer.

In the guided interview the interviewer has before him a carefully selected list of questions, each aimed at bringing out some facet of the candidate's character, past experience, approach to work, sociability and the like, the questions following logically on from each other.

It is as well, in the guided interview, if few notes are made of the candidate's answers until after he has left the room. We all have an inherent distrust of anyone taking down in writing what we say and we tend, on such occasions, to be stilted and ill at ease. The interviewer will, then, memorise as much as he can and enter up the answers later.

In the unguided interview the candidate is encouraged to talk, not necessarily about the specific job in view but about himself, his likes, dislikes, hobbies, interests and his general background. From this spate of words, the interviewer builds up a mental picture of the candidate as he would be if employed by the firm.

For the interviewer lacking experience, the guided method is probably the more reliable. The questions to be asked can be worked out by several brains and the answers, likewise, can be judged by several people, thus relieving the interviewer of sole responsibility for the final decision.

On the other hand, the really skilled interviewer will probably prefer the unguided method as he will feel constricted by the question and answer method. He will have learnt to rely on his judgement and to discount the effects of anxiety on the part of the candidate.

Both methods are good, both are widely used, but, whatever the method, it is of supreme importance that the interviewer shall have in his mind a clear and detailed picture of the actual job for which he is interviewing the candidate. Unless he has, in other words, a clear knowledge of the shape of the hole to be filled, he cannot possibly tell whether the peg will fit. This is important.

Even so, mere technical knowledge of mechanical requirements and classified aptitudes does not, of itself, make an interviewer into a good interviewer. Much more is needed.

Far more important than what the candidate says, is what the candidate is in a three-dimensional sense. We each have a soul, a mind and a body and unless each of these is matched to the job and environment, an ill-fit will result. The trained interviewer is well aware of this fact and will use his powers of discernment to form a mental picture of the candidate in all his three aspects. Most people attending an interview are nervous; they are conscious that their future destiny may hang on the case they can make out for themselves; they are anxious to impress: they are even prone at times to lay claim to qualities they do not possess if, by so doing, they think they can enhance their chances of acceptance.

These nerves affect different people in different ways. Some will come prepared with almost a speech of self-adulation only to forget every word of it and thus present a picture of tongue-tied misery. Others, more self-confident but not necessarily more suitable, may achieve a measure of high pressure self-salesmanship through which it is difficult indeed for the interviewer to penetrate. Between these extremes lies the usual range of variants, all possessing one common factor. The candidate being interviewed seldom presents more than a superficial resemblance to the sort of person he really is. The interviewer, it follows, must possess the capacity for seeing below the surface to the real character before him, the character which is to be weighed and tested.

This capacity can only be acquired by a combination of interviewing experience and a deep understanding of human-ity based on wide reading and contact with life as it is lived at all levels. Only thus equipped can the interviewer discern the essential character of the candidate before him.

Not only must the interviewer possess this sympathetic understanding, he must also be able to project it so that the candidate, however nervous, is himself conscious of it. Recognising it, he will respond by talking more freely and more intimately, disclosing perhaps something of his ambitions, desires, hopes, interests and antipathies as they really are, and not as he thinks the demands of the offered job require that they should be. He will be frank when he feels he is understood and in the presence of a sympathetic mind.

In any large firm, and in many smaller ones, these frank disclosures of apparently irrelevant matters can be turned to substantial account by the astute interviewer. It is true that he will have in mind one vacancy to be filled and the suitability of the candidate for that specific vacancy will be his first consideration. At the same time, however, he will know that other vacancies will occur in the future and he will, with this knowledge, be on the watch for any evidence of any special ability such as linguistic ; any special interest such as electricity ; any special vocation such as accounting or management. Where these are present, he will consider carefully whether it might not be in the best interests of his firm to take on the candidate for grooming in preparation for subsequent vacancies likely to occur.

Interviewing is far from being a hit or miss process though no one would claim that it is, or will ever be, an exact science. This is because the interviewer himself is possessed of opinions, convictions and other characteristics which, however much he may try to avoid it, cannot help but colour his judgments of others. That the interviewer shall be as impartial as possible is all-important since he is the buyer of the most important raw material any factory or office ever spends money on—skill and brains.

But management can't neglect psychology at the point when the candidate has been matched to the vacancy. To do so would be to nullify all the complex process involved in his selection.

The candidate, or new employee as he now is, must be set to work, encouraged to work hard, trained, groomed for promotion and, in the words of the Factories Act, provision must be made for his health, safety and welfare. Condensed, this means that he must be studied as an individual, cared for, allowed to develop his innate and acquired characteristics and never allowed to become just another number on the clock.

There was a phase in management thinking, a phase now fortunately recognised as misguided, in which it was held that men and machines were comparable. It was possible, the argument ran, to assess the capacity, capabilities and short-comings of men and machines in like terms. Just as certain machines could do some jobs best, so could some men ; just as machines could break down with overwork, so could men ; just as machines ultimately wore out or became obsolete, so did men. Why, then, it was asked, bother about all this special care for the human element ?

The fallacy, of course, was at least three-fold. First, a machine's capacity can be seen at a glance and is clearly detailed in the maker's handbook ; not so that of a man.

Secondly, like machines have a like performance and can be relied upon to give that performance at any time. This is not true of men. Thirdly, and most important, no machine has the remotest interest in what machines are working on either side of it or in the same room. This is totally untrue of men, who react markedly and actively to their colleagues and neighbours.

It thus behoves any firm to study carefully the individual characters of those whom it employs ; it should study them not only as individuals but also in their relationship to each other. Many a factory or work-room of contented workers has been disrupted from the foreman downwards by the introduction of one new employee, himself quite a harmless character but, as events have proved, temperamentally out of harmony with his new colleagues. It may be impossible to foresee this, but the first evidence of it will, to the wise management, be the signal for a transfer of the misfit employee. Characters, then, must be studied not only singly but also in terms of their emotional impact on each other.

One further factor of great importance in the ultimate well-being of the new employee and, by hypothesis, of the whole firm is the need to let him develop, and help him to develop, his sense of vocation.

Some knowledge of what this vocation is should have emerged at interview ; it should not be forgotten. Even if that vocation may not materially be of benefit to the employee in his job he will, if frustrated, become difficult to handle and eventually impossible to employ. Every effort must therefore be made to see that he has opportunity for study, guidance where he needs it and ultimately, if it can be arranged, a transfer to work in which he can give expression to his calling.

If no such work can be found within the firm, then it is probably better to tell the employee so and, if he wishes, let him go elsewhere. The only alternative is likely to be a frustrated, dissatisfied man of little use to the firm or to himself and a source of unrest within the working community.

Although, primarily. an employee is considered to work

for money, this is far less than the truth. In addition to income, he wants status, prospects and a sense of being wanted and needed in the job he is doing. Most of all, he wants justice as between himself and his fellow employees. This being so, the psychologist—the man who knows and understands these natural desires and aspirations—has quite as big an influence on the well-being of the employee as does the man who sanctions his pay cheque.

There is a marked psychological aspect to be considered in the matter of financial incentives, attitude to work, proneness to accident, reaction to supervision, time keeping, health and absenteeism. Many of these matters, in their practical aspect, are discussed elsewhere in this book but the reader must not lose sight of the psychological implications which also attend them. At no point in the direction of human activities can the teachings of psychology be disregarded.

CHAPTER V

Management and Finance

With this chapter we now start to examine in some detail each in turn of the functions of management. You will remember that these are distribution—or selling—production, finance, development and personnel relations.

You will also remember that it is not the job of the chief executive to be himself a fully qualified specialist in each of these functions. Apart from anything else, he couldn't be, as the proper study of each would take a lifetime.

No, what the chief executive must be able to do is understand sufficient of the capabilities and uses of each function of management to enable him to use it to its maximum capacity. He must, in other words, know where each function fits into the management picture, know what to ask of each functional head and be able to read and interpret the results of action taken by each functional head.

We are going to start this series of chapters, then, by dealing with the function of finance.

I don't want to imply by this that finance is any more or less important than any other function; to do so would be to suggest that the pendulum of a grandfather clock was more important than the escapement. All functions are equally important and each has its rightful part to play in good management.

The financial function, it may be mentioned for the record, is known as the function of conservation—a name easily remembered if it be realised that the main object of the functional head in charge of finance is to conserve the assets of the company. Unless these be conserved they will waste and continuous wastage of assets leads in but one direction, to but one inescapable result.

Perhaps the most easily appreciated illustration of the place of finance in industry is afforded by describing it as the life-blood of the company.

The body cannot continue without blood and will suffer distress if there be too much or too little relative to need. The " pressure " must be kept constant.

In terms of industry this means that there shall be adequate capital to finance current needs, to provide against contingencies and to permit of reasonable development in accordance with planned policy.

If there be too much capital, interest will be paid on idle money ; if there be too little, current business will be fettered and no development will be possible other than on a hand-to-mouth, casual and occasional basis.

Financial control, therefore, or the maintenance of constant pressure, is much more than a matter of double-entry book-keeping and it is necessary to discuss those matters which the manager needs to know when using, or in liaison with, the financial function.

Control of income can be substantially excluded from our deliberations since income is only remotely controllable. Control of expenditure, though, is clearly the direct concern of management.

In theory, not a penny can be spent without the sanction of the directors who represent the shareholders who own the money. This is logical and sound, but considerations of common sense dictate that the theory must be modified. Authority to spend money must be delegated.

The Board will reserve to itself some spending authority, such as that on major development projects, vast advertising campaigns and the like but, outside the range of such matters, authority to spend will be delegated to the managing director and, through him, to less-senior personnel.

However able a managing director, he will not want to be bothered, nor should he be bothered, to sanction every item of expenditure. Many are too small for his direct attention— but not too small for attention ; others, again, can only be assessed as to their true worth by someone in much closer touch with the reason for them. In this category I put the expenses of a salesman in a large firm. The sales manager will know whether they are justified by past or potential future returns to the firm but it is no part of the managing director's job to concern himself with details of that nature. The sales manager is responsible for this function and, as has already been said, he must have delegated to him the authority to sanction such expenditure as he needs to enable him to do his job.

So it goes on, responsibility being linked with authority to incur expenditure right down the line till, at the end, we find, perhaps, the office boy with the tea-money for which he must account weekly to his immediate superior.

It is appropriate now to consider the difference between capital and revenue expenditure—a distinction which should be, but all too often is not, clear to anyone with any power to spend any money other than his own.

Capital expenditure is that devoted to items of a capital nature by which the assets of the company are, however slightly, increased. For example, a new machine, a new building, a door-knob for the board room or a slide rule for the drawing office are all items of a capital nature.

Revenue expenditure, however, is that incurred in connection with the day-to-day running of the business—stamps, telephone, wages, salaries, for instance, none of which increases the assets of the business but without which the business could not continue.

Try to get this clear. Name one or two items of company expense that occur to you at random and then reason out whether they are capital or revenue items.

It may help you to clear up any obscure cases if you remember that items of revenue expense find their way to the Trading and Profit and Loss Accounts, while items of capital expense, since they are the assets of the business, are not written off completely each year. Depreciation only is written off, the asset itself remaining on the books.

Depreciation, in name, anyway, is moderately well understood, but the theory on which it is based may not be quite so familiar. As it is a very important matter when discussing finance, I shall consider it here in some detail.

Everything in nature is subject to a wasting process, only the speed of which varies. There is nothing which, if left untended for a long period, would not deteriorate with the passing years. This applies alike to human beings, buildings, machinery, furniture.

It applies also, of course, to leases and to patents which have a life fixed in advance and which expire at the end of that period, thus becoming worthless.

Now the assets of a business comprise many things; those listed and countless others, all of which are gradually becoming worn out, less valuable or—and this is a new factor—obsolete. Wise management cannot possibly ignore this.

Two steps, therefore, are taken to deal with the unavoidable situation with which management is confronted; these steps are maintenance and depreciation.

Clearly, in many cases, careful maintenance can help to preserve the asset. This applies to buildings and machinery particularly but not at all, of course, to leases and patents.

Even careful maintenance, however, cannot indefinitely prolong the life of an asset nor, to any great extent, can it prevent an asset becoming obsolete.

Consequently, it is necessary to reduce the book value of the assets year by year with the object of reducing that value to zero at the same moment that the asset becomes valueless to the company. This is ideal in theory, but, of course, is seldom actually realised except in the case of assets with a fixed, known life.

It would be wrong to reduce all the assets by a fixed percentage per annum; each asset must be judged independently, its life estimated and possible obsolescence allowed for. This done, means can be devised for writing down the value annually; of these means there are several in general use.

First, and simplest, is the method used for depreciating the assets in what are called the extractive industries—coal-mining, for instance. Here a technical estimate is made of the total tonnage of coal likely to be won from the mine and depreciation is directly related to the tonnage actually won in the relevant year.

Secondly, another simple method can be applied to leases, patents and assets of fixed and known life. In the case of leases on property, the amount paid for the lease can be divided by the number of years it has to run and the amount thus calculated written off the value year by year until, when the lease expires, it has no value in the books.

In the case of patents, which sometimes acquire substantial value to a company, a similar process can be adopted though notice must be taken of the possibility that the patent may be superseded by a competitor before its full life has expired. If this is at all probable, it is wiser to write off the value over a shorter term of years to guard against such an eventuality.

Fixtures and fittings seldom represent any great value in the books and can be written down each year by a fixed percentage based on an arbitrarily assessed replacement period.

This brings us to the biggest problem, that of machinery and plant which is becoming out of date, wearing out and incurring more and more maintenance expenditure as the years go by. Further, its rate of wearing out depends on the amount of use it gets, but the speed with which it becomes obsolete is governed by little more than pure chance and the possible invention of more modern equipment.

No management can assess accurately the life of any of its machinery unless it be special-purpose machinery bought for one particular contract; this so seldom happens that we needn't consider it as a complication. Management must reason intelligently and base its depreciation rates on the conclusions it reaches.

It may be estimated that one machine will not wear out under normal conditions for ten years but there may be a likelihood that it will be superseded by a more modern and faster-working model in five years. Another machine, very fast running, may have an estimated life of six years with little expectation that it will become obsolete. Yet another, seldom used, perhaps, may be considered to have a life of twenty years while still other machinery may be virtually obsolete already.

Each of these machines, and all the others, must be considered separately and an effective life assessed, this effective life being the period during which, in management's view, the machine will constitute an asset to the business. It will also be necessary to decide on the approximate scrap value of the machine at the end of its effective life, since the difference between value now and scrap value in due course will be the sum to be written off the value over the period of the effective life. Not, admittedly, an easy sum to calculate, but one that must be calculated as accurately as possible in the case of every machine.

Having decided the sum to be written off and the number of years over which it is to be written off, two methods are available for carrying out the process.

The first, and simpler, method is to deal with the problem as with leases and patents and write off each year an amount calculated by dividing the sum to be written off by the number of years. This, however, has the disadvantage that the asset is depreciated by a fixed sum each year whereas, in fact, a machine depreciates in value much more in its early years than it does when it is old; the method, therefore, is not consistent with reality.

The second method avoids this criticism. Each year a fixed percentage is written off the book value of the machine, the actual amount written off becoming, of course, smaller each year.

Thus, if a machine valued new at £16,000 is to be written down to a value of £900 over a period of fifteen years, the procedure will be to write off $17\frac{1}{2}$ per cent each year from the diminishing value. In round figures, this would mean writing off £2,800 in the first year, £2,310 in the second year and so on until, in the last year, the sum to be written off would be just under £200.

The advantages of this method are obvious. It bears a close relationship to reality in that depreciation is taken at diminishing figures and in that the larger sums to be written off fall in the years when the machine is new and its earning capacity probably at a maximum. Further, in the latter years of the machine's life depreciation will be low while maintenance costs for repairs are likely to be high.

It is important to note here that depreciation is a very vital and necessary book-keeping process but it does not, of itself, provide the money to replace the asset which is being depreciated. Depreciation is thus not an end in itself, it is a means to an essential end.

The effect of writing off sums in respect of depreciation is, of course, to reduce the net profit earned by the company; this must be so as depreciation represents a wasting away, or diminishing value, of an asset. It does not follow automatically though that a fund is created out of which assets can be replaced. Such a fund, or savings account, must be specially created. It is then called a Reserve or a Sinking Fund.

There are several ways in which these reserves can be established, the simplest being the mere setting aside of annual sums in a separate account to be used for replacements.

This, however, is neither a very practical nor a very realistic way of achieving the desired end. Much better is it to invest a sum each year such that, at compound interest, the accumulated total will provide for the replacement of the asset at the end of its effective life. In this way money is not left idle and a smaller annual sum can be set aside each year than would otherwise be the case.

Companies will often have recourse to an insurance company for this purpose, especially where assets of fixed, known life are concerned. The procedure is simply to take out a Sinking Fund policy which will accrue to the total sum required in the set number of years, in return for a fixed annual premium, quoted in advance by the insurance company.

Depreciation, then, recognises that an asset has a diminishing value and is the process by which that diminution is measured. Reserves are the means adopted to ensure that money will be available to replace the asset when its life is expired.

It is far from unusual, of course, for companies to use the system of reserves for purchases other than the replacement of assets. Reserve accounts can be set up, for example, to meet possible contingencies, unassessable tax liabilities, future development programmes or for general purposes, just as the responsible householder will save up in good times in order to be able to meet his obligations in the uncertain future.

Mention has been made several times in the course of this chapter to various ledger accounts and other book-keeping matters and it has been assumed that the reader will be generally familiar with the subject. Should this assumption be over-optimistic in some cases, a copy of *Teach Yourself Book-keeping* will provide the necessary background knowledge.

Briefly, the purpose of the Trading and Profit and Loss Accounts is to show, at the credit, the income from sales and, at the debit, to list all those items of revenue expenditure which have been incurred in earning the income. Adjustment is made, of course, for varying levels of stock and work in progress and the balance at the debit is the net profit earned by the company. Despite small variations in detail favoured by different accountants, all Trading and Profit and Loss Accounts conform to this general pattern.

It will not, I think, have escaped notice that these accounts can, by their nature, afford great assistance to management to whom has been delegated so much authority to incur revenue expenditure. They provide, in fact, a list of all that expenditure, and, by so doing, present a picture of all items in their proper perspective relative to each other and to the income achieved. It is not surprising then that management studies these accounts keenly in its attempt to control expenditure.

Unfortunately, Trading and Profit and Loss Accounts, as usually presented, are subject to two faults which, together, reduce substantially their value as aids to management.

The first of these faults is that they are not usually available until some months after the period to which they relate, by which time it is difficult, if not impossible, to apply effectively any control. Secondly, the items of expense are usually given collectively under general headings such as depreciation, rent, salaries, lighting and the like, split up only as between the factories in the Trading Account and all other headings in the Profit and Loss Account. This affords little help to the management looking for a detailed and positive method of expense control, unless each item be analysed down to its component parts. It is not very useful, for example, to know that salaries have risen unless one also knows whether the increase has been general or confined to one specific department, in which case the increase can be considered in relation to the results achieved thereby.

To meet these two objections, management is increasingly adopting two measures, the one designed to provide prompt accounts at frequent intervals and the other to show expense items in detailed form so arranged as to be more easily controlled in relation to income.

The former expedient, prompt and frequent accounts, will be more suitably dealt with in the next chapter ; the second is known as the Sales Pound method of expense control.

It is safe to assume that the majority of businesses have been in existence for some years and that past records of income and expenditure are available ; it is on these records and their intelligent interpretation that the Sales Pound method is based.

The first stage in developing the method is to analyse past records and decide within the closest possible limits what proportion of each pound of sales income should reasonably be spent on (a) producing the article sold, (b) selling the article and (c) administering the business ; the remainder of the pound will, of course, be profit.

Assessing figures in such detail as this is not nearly so difficult as it sounds and its comparative simplicity will surprise many who have not tried hitherto to use their past records for detailed expense control purposes. Further, complete accuracy is neither possible nor necessary; once the method is in being, it will increase in accuracy year by year.

We will assume, then, that past evidence shows that, of every pound of sales income, 12s. 6d. (62½p) will be absorbed by manufacturing costs, 5s. 0d. (25p) by selling and advertising costs, 6d. (2½p) by the costs of administering the business. The remaining 2s. 0d. (10p) will be the profit earned.

With this decision taken, the Trading and Profit and Loss Accounts are replaced in the accounting system by three separate accounts devoted respectively to Production, Distribution and Administration Profit and Loss and one final Profit and Loss Account.

To the credit of each of these accounts are posted the calculated percentages of sales income—in our example these are 62½ per cent to production, 25 per cent to distribution, 2½ per cent to administration and 10 per cent to the final account.

At the debit, each of the first three of these accounts takes all the items of expenditure directly incurred in connection with the process to which the account relates. Thus, to production are posted all factory expenses including materials, wages, depreciation on plant and factory buildings, rent of factory, salaries paid for factory supervisors.

To distribution go all the expenses incurred in the selling side of the business such as rent of sales office, agent's commission, salesmen's expenses and salaries and advertising costs.

The administration account takes, in effect, all the remaining items of expense including rent of general office, salaries of clerical staff employed in administration, directors' fees, accountants' fees, depreciation on general office buildings and furniture, again to name but a few.

It will be seen that if the original breaking-down of the sales pound has been accurate, the total expenses in each account will balance exactly with the proportion of sales income in each case, and this should be the aim.

Any big difference between debit and credit items in any

of these three accounts will show at once either that the estimated proportion of sales income is wrong or that the expenses have risen or fallen to an extent greater than was anticipated. Further, it will show this under the appropriate heading—production, distribution or administration.

Until the method has been in use for a few years it is quite likely that the estimated proportions of income will need adjustment. Thereafter, unless some major change takes place, this will remain practically static and any large balance on either side of these accounts will call for immediate action on the part of management. Unlike the Trading and Profit and Loss Account system, however, the Sales Pound method will show up precisely where that action should be taken, thus providing a close measure of financial control.

It remains to mention the Final Profit and Loss Account, to which, in our example, was credited 10 per cent of the sales turnover.

This account accepts the balances from the other three accounts, cross-posted, of course, from debit to credit or credit to debit and the balance on the Final Profit and Loss Account is the net profit of the business.

Intelligently used, the Sales Pound method of financial control is an invaluable asset to the manager, obliged, as he is, to accept responsibility from the Board to spend money and to delegate that authority to his subordinates ; delegation of such authority would be a dangerous proceeding without an adequate check as to the way in which it was being used or abused.

CHAPTER VI

Management and Costing

The computer age has made possible "instant-accounting"
in that, given appropriate programming, it is practicable to
produce a complete set of accounts at any time. Even so,
only the largest companies can indulge in this luxury. By
far the majority are still committed to the old systems in
which accountants' figures, often submitted months after the
period to which they relate, are not a great deal of use to the
manager who wants to be up to date, taking decisions
promptly and basing them on as much information as possible. By use of the Sales Pound method of presentation, it
is possible to exercise intelligent expense control, but even
this is not enough.

To-day, business moves at a fast pace, methods and
conditions change rapidly and competition is becoming ever
keener ; to keep abreast of all this, the modern manager must
be kept constantly informed of what is happening and what
is likely to happen. Cost accounting provides this service.

I have said already, several times, that there's no magic in
management ; it is the ultimate objective of cost accounting
to see that there's no guesswork either.

It is beyond the scope of this work to include detailed
instruction for the installation and operation of a costing
system and, further, it is not a part of management to
concern itself with the mechanics of costing any more than
the mechanics of production. Provided that the manager
knows what demands to make on his costing service and how
to read the results submitted to him, he can well leave the
ways and means to the man who has to do the job.

The cost accountant works on the theory that every penny
spent by a company is spent for a purpose, that every item
of expenditure is authorised somewhere and is attributable
to some means of furthering the company's interests. The
financial accountant, of course, thinks on similar lines but he

is less interested in precisely why every penny is spent, and he does not concern himself with the detailed relationship between money spent and work produced. Cost accounts, therefore, must not be confused with financial accounts, though both originate with the same basic figures and each should be reconciled with the other periodically.

It is also a characteristic of financial accountants that they practise positive accuracy all through their work, requiring every account to balance exactly and every penny to be accounted for. In this, they are, of course, doing their job properly and their figures would serve little useful purpose otherwise.

On the other hand, the cost accountant, while himself a believer in accuracy, realises that it is his job to keep management promptly and frequently informed of what is happening, how policy decisions are working out, whether profits are being made and where they are being made. He realises, too, that promptitude and frequency are incompatible with complete accuracy when applied to the income and expenditure of a manufacturing concern.

The cost accountant, therefore, must submit to management monthly or quarterly reports and accounts which are sufficiently accurate for managerial purposes but which must, by their nature, lack the complete accuracy of the financial accounts submitted less frequently and less promptly.

These regular reports will show management, for example, the estimated net profit made during the preceding period, the many headings of expenditure and how much has been expended under each, the profits and losses made by all the departments, factories or processes, the cost of service departments, such as maintenance, the cost of idle time, lost time, bad time-keeping, machine break-downs and hold-ups in production. On request, the cost accountant will submit special reports dealing with, perhaps, the profitability or otherwise of one particular contract or process. In short, his purpose is to supply all the financial details analysed in such a way that management can see, almost daily, where its activities are leading the company. This aid to navigation cannot be adequately provided by the financial accounts of the company.

What has been said applies mainly to management at top level though the cost accountant's services are available, and valuable, to management at all levels. The foreman or chargehand, for example, can be supplied with details concerning the efficiency, or otherwise, of his department or section, showing the difference between actual and possible efficiency and, what is more useful still, what steps he should take to bring the two into closer agreement.

Heads of departments can call on the cost accountant to supply estimated costs of new methods, proposed changes and any other projects, the expediency of which they are considering.

To do all this the cost accountant has to indulge in a wealth of detail and some intelligent forecasting, his object being to prepare a budget of expenditure for the ensuing year, detailed under as many separate headings as he can distinguish. This list in itself, of course, is immensely valuable to management when compared, eventually, with actual expenditure incurred under each heading.

Taking the budget as his guide, the cost accountant next groups his items under the department where each originates and thereby brings into being an expense charge likely to be incurred by each department in the year ahead. The departments so treated will not include only the productive ones, of course ; they will include also administrative and service departments, sales, personnel and research departments and, in fact, all the departments into which the firm is capable of being divided.

In so grouping the expenses, the cost accountant will have recourse, in many cases, to what is known as apportionment, or the splitting up of single items of expense over more than one department on some agreed basis such that each department bears its true share of the expenses.

The next stage will be the distribution of all expenditure, other than administration, on non-productive departments by apportioning a fair share to each productive department.

The cost accountant now has a list of productive departments each charged with a fair share of all the expenses of the business other than administration. It is his job at this point to establish a means whereby all these expenses will be recovered in the cost of the articles manufactured.

To make this possible he must draw up, or have provided for him by management, a budgeted forecast of total output for the year, preferably in terms of running hours of each machine in each productive department.

After making sundry allowances to compensate for difference in size and value between individual machines, the cost accountant is in a position to state how much it will cost to run each machine for one hour. This hourly rate will include all productive and non-productive expenses incurred.

Admittedly, this is a considerable over-simplification of a cost accountant's work, but I have included in my description sufficient detail to enable the manager to appreciate the basis of costing.

As we have already proved that, in nearly every case, it is the economic price that decides cost it might justly be argued that there is not really a great deal of point in calculating cost in such meticulous detail ; this indeed might have some measure of truth in it if, in fact, the cost accountant considered his work finished when he had made his calculations and set up his hourly rates. On the contrary, he considers that his work is then just starting.

There are as many individual methods of factory documentation—or paper work—as there are individual factories, but one feature is common to all with any claim to efficiency —the recording of materials used and time spent on each job by each man and machine.

By routing this information through the cost accountant's hands, details of the greatest value to management can be extracted and presented in acceptable form.

No manager has time to worry through a welter of production details nor, in most cases, could he draw a conclusive opinion as to the results of what he had read : on the other hand, every manager must know what is going on, what effect is being given to his instructions and how the pre-arranged policy is developing.

It is the cost accountant's province to supply this information without indulging in too much detail. If he can submit accounts and reports that give a true general picture of the company's progress, any point requiring greater elaboration can be the subject of a special analysis on demand.

From the production details passing through the cost accountant's office, and from his own knowledge of the constituent parts of each hourly rate, the cost accountant will supply management with all details of lost time and the reasons therefor, with indications of material wastage, with efficiency ratios applicable to each department, with comparisons between estimated expenditure and actual, and between estimates and actual costs of jobs or contracts, with analyses showing the profitability or otherwise of separate jobs and, in addition to all this, an estimated profit and loss account applicable to the company as a whole.

Even this does not exhaust the potentialities of a competent costing system. It often happens that management is considering alternative courses of action ; whether or not, for example, to install a new machine.

Here again the cost accountant can help by setting up an imaginary hourly rate for the machine and relating this to a past period, thereby showing what would have been the general effect of having had the machine. With this available, management's decision is much more easy to take.

Remember that it is not only the chief executive or even the department heads who benefit from the cost accountant's services. Foremen, too, can be materially helped in their management work if they be told, monthly or weekly, the difference between what their sections have done and what they could have done under best possible conditions. Since reports of this nature should always include enough detail for the foreman to see where the short-fall occurred, the steps to be taken towards improvement are clearly visible.

To summarise the work of the cost accountant, it can be said that his task is to keep management at all levels in constant touch with what is happening in the works, however complex, and in the administration of the company as a whole and to relate these events to the furtherance of company policy. In short, the cost accountant reduces guesswork to its absolute minimum.

To realise the importance of this service, imagine for a moment a managing director of a concern comprising some ten separate factories, all busily making articles of different kinds in widely differing quantities and qualities. Clearly, even if he had no other work to do and could spend his time walking through the factories, he could never get a true idea of what progress his company was making, of which were the most profitable lines or of the real reasons for lost production.

Now give him the accounts and reports we have been discussing. At once he can see that No. 3 factory is losing time because of material shortages and that No. 4 is handicapped by plant inefficiencies. He can see, too, that the proportion of rejects went up substantially in the preceding month; that No. 6 factory is running at 65 per cent efficiency whereas all the others are over 75 per cent; that over the whole company there is a tendency to over-estimate production costs; that the line which he considered most profitable was, in fact, barely paying its way. Finally, with his estimated profit and loss account, he is in a position to see the effect of all this on the financial progress of the company.

For the able manager, a short note asking for elaboration of a few figures would be the only action necessary before taking positive steps to eradicate the shortcomings.

Sometimes, of course, concerns with many factories have them in various parts of the country and separate costing systems have to be set up for each.

Though this may make the work of the cost accountant more complex, it need not in any way reduce the value of the information submitted to management. The cost accountant will adopt a method known as Uniform Costing, by which the apportionment and distribution of expenditure will be applied on a uniform basis, thereby rendering directly comparable all production returns whatever their source within the widespread activities of the business.

The most enlightened managements are not even content with these services and require from the cost accountant even more assistance still, in the form of standard costs.

These are product costs, hypothetically calculated on the assumption that a certain level of turnover will be maintained and that certain expenditure will be incurred in the year ahead. By comparing the actual costs with the standard costs, variances are indications of a departure from the pre-arranged plan and give rise at once to investigation of the cause.

Once a system of standard costs is in being, of course, the way is open for the introduction of full budgetary control, which is not such a frightening technique as it may sound.

It merely means that the whole schedule of production and sales is laid down a year ahead and all expenses to be incurred in producing a certain volume of sales are budgeted in advance.

Each department is told first what will be required of it and is asked what it will need to spend, under all headings, to enable it to carry out its task. These budgets are then reconciled, scaled up or down and adjusted until a complete total budget of sales and expenditure is reached.

The head of each department is then given authority to spend the agreed sums and is required to play his agreed part, application only being made to higher management for permission to depart from the budget.

In effect, the whole subsequent year's transactions are thus planned in advance and management is freed from day-to-day worries.

I must make it clear, though, that budgetary control calls for management and planning of a very high order and is applicable in its full sense only to those firms in which the Board initiates production. It could not well apply, for instance, to the firm dependent on customers for its daily production programme though, even in these firms, some measure of budgetary control is not impossible.

It remains to say something of the accuracy of costing figures which, by their very nature and the need for promptitude, must contain a certain amount of forecasting. We have seen, for instance, that the incidence of overhead expenses is calculated on a predicted level of production.

It might be held that this feature made cost accounts of little value and thereby destroyed most of their benefit to management.

It is true, of course, that cost figures do contain certain intelligent forecasts and it is also true that if these forecasts were very wide of the mark the cost figures would be correspondingly false, but that is not the end.

Every year the financial books of the company are audited and, when this is done, actual income and expenditure items are disclosed. Further, both financial and cost books are based, in the ultimate, on the same items of income and expenditure.

If, then, at the end of each year, the cost figures are brought into line with the financial figures, the extent of any such adjustment can be seen and a basis is provided on which to make the forecasts for the ensuing year.

It is therefore customary for a reconciliation account to be raised at each financial accounting period. To this account are posted the actual items of expense incurred and the forecast items used for costing purposes.

The balance on this account will indicate the margin of error in the cost accounts and, if added to, or subtracted from, the profit or loss estimated by the cost accountant will bring this figure into agreement with that calculated by the company's auditor ; further, by knowing the margin of error, and its origins, the forecast for the next ensuing year can be much more accurately laid down.

Thus a costing system with provision for reconciliation with the financial books is likely to achieve ever-increasing accuracy.

CHAPTER VII

The Manager as Statistician

In the last chapter we saw how means were devised by which the manager, whether chief executive or of less exalted stature, could be provided with statistical information relative to his task. Providing the information, however, is one thing ; interpreting it is quite another.

The manager who is to be given any worth-while information on a host of financial and other matters must expect to receive this in the form of reports in which figures will play a substantial part ; he is unlikely to be very successful unless he brings to bear a critical and understanding mind. He must be something, in short, of a statistician.

A statistician is defined as one who studies numerical facts collected systematically and arranged ; it does not follow that he must of necessity be a high-powered professor living in the realms of theory. In fact, the manager-statistician must be the opposite, a realist, conscious that he can benefit by a study of theory but never allowing theories to blind his mind to facts.

The first thing a manager must do, then, when presented with a report containing numerous figures is to arrange these figures so that they become immediately comparable.

As an example, assume that the manager has called for, and received, a survey of sales, gross profits and net profits taken at monthly intervals during the preceding three years, annotated with reasons for rises and falls.

This is not by any means an unusual demand for a manager to make and he may make it to his sales manager, his cost accountant or his accountant. If the individual called upon be himself a good statistician, the report will be in tabular form or will contain a table of figures as an appendix. All too often, however, such reports are made in paragraph form peppered with figures in such a way that, at first reading, it is almost impossible to follow the reasoning or, in fact, to learn anything useful at all.

The manager who receives such a report, therefore, must either send it back for tabulation or tabulate it himself. This, in the case stated in the example, is not difficult.

Tabulation consists of extracting the figures from the body of the report and so arranging them in columns that each can be compared with the other. All that is required is a sheet of ruled paper, containing, in this case, four columns.

In the first, or left-hand, column the month and date are entered ; the remaining three take, respectively, figures of sales, gross profit and net profit. Thus arranged, the text of the report can be read intelligently and, by reference to the prepared table, comparisons can be made and ratios calculated to any required extent.

Tabulation, then, should be applied to any series of figures calling for easy comparison but, at times, even tabulation cannot present as clear a picture as is required.

To carry the example further, let us suppose that, once supplied with the sales and profit details already mentioned, the manager wants to investigate seasonal changes. To do this he will have to run his eye down the table of figures, watching their rise and fall and carrying in his mind a variety of different factors. This, to an able manager well grounded in statistics, is not impossible but, if frequent reference is to be made, a much simpler means can be provided by charting the figures.

The object of a chart is to supply a means of at-a-glance reference ; to make visible, as it were, the variations between different figures without requiring feats of memory, calculation or judgement.

The preparation of a chart is not a complicated matter and the procedure will be familiar to many.

Squared paper will be required if the chart is to carry detailed figures and it is as well to use paper ruled at ten lines to the inch.

The horizontal axis of the paper is marked off in dates—months, in our example—and the vertical axis in values, the lowest at the bottom and progressing upwards in constant steps. The range of values should be such as to contain within it any possible figures likely to occur on the chart.

Having prepared the chart, it remains only to put in the ordinates. This is done by making a mark at a spot on the chart which is immediately to the right of the figure to be entered and perpendicularly above the month to which it refers. After treating all the figures in this way, the ordinates are connected up by a continuous line running through each of them.

In our example, this will result in three separate lines—or curves—one relating to sales, one to gross profit and one to net profit. If different-coloured inks be used for each, the last possibility of confusion will be removed.

The chart will then consist of three lines, rising and falling in peaks and valleys as they pass across the chart. A rise will indicate an increase and a fall a decrease. With all three on the one chart, instant comparisons can be made and the reasons for unexplained phenomena can be investigated.

Finally, by arranging to have this chart kept up to date each month, the manager is provided with a continuous picture of the sales activities of the business.

The man at the top, though, must interest himself in a number of other figures besides sales and he will probably apply the chart method to these as well—value of production charted with productive wages paid, monthly costs per unit of various standard lines, indirect wages with productive wages—these are but three possible bases for charts, but a word of warning must be given.

Too many people new to management fall into the temptation of charting for the sake of charting. Sooner or later they find that they have defeated their own object. Admittedly, at first glance, a wall full of highly-coloured charts does give an appearance of high-pressure efficiency but charts are not a substitute for efficiency, they are one of the means by which efficiency is achieved and must never be allowed to exceed that function.

Before deciding to add another chart to his collection, then, the manager must be completely satisfied that it will perform a really useful task, that it will be an aid to his deliberations and that it will not merely fill up an unsightly space on the wall.

I have confined my description entirely, so far, to line charts as these are the most useful as aids to management. There are, however, other sorts, of which two in particular deserve mention, the bar chart and the pie chart.

The bar chart is mainly used for the purpose of comparing performance with a pre-arranged task; one might be used, for example, by a works manager who wished to have before him a ready means of comparing actual production with planned production.

In such a case, the horizontal lines on the chart would indicate units of production, vertical lines indicating the dates. The space between any two vertical lines, therefore, would indicate the number of units scheduled for production between the two dates.

By drawing a horizontal line, or bar, across the chart as each day's production is known, comparison of actual with scheduled output can be seen at a glance.

The pie chart is of little use for direct managerial purposes but it has a considerable use when management wishes to inform its workers of statistical matters relating to the business.

As its name implies, the completed chart has the appearance of a pie, looked at from above, the appropriate information being conveyed by means of segments of varying sizes drawn in and, preferably, coloured.

In order to prepare a pie chart, the various items of information to be shown are first reduced to percentages of the whole. Thus, if the object of the chart be to show the workers the proportions of turnover devoted to direct wages, raw materials, overhead expenses and profit, these items, taken from the firm's accounts, are first expressed as percentages of the total.

A circle is then drawn, representing either total turnover or a sales pound, and segments are drawn within it representing the items listed above.

The drawing of the segments proportionately presents no difficulty if the diameter is first drawn in. The percentages are then applied to 360—the number of degrees in a circle—and the resultant figures are considered as degrees of angle. A schoolroom protractor is the only equipment needed.

Each segment is then proportionately larger or smaller than its neighbours and the extent to which any one factor differs from the others is immediately visible even to those with no knowledge at all of figures, charts, statistics or management.

So far, we have considered charts only as a means of providing graphical representation of historical facts ; they have, in addition, an even greater use as foundations on which to base future predictions.

Anyone with even a moderate experience of management will agree that his job would be simplified beyond measure if only he could see to-day what is going to happen to-morrow. Indeed, without a very good idea of what is likely to happen to-morrow, management would be almost impossible.

It thus behoves management at all levels, and particularly at top level, to bring to bear all its resources in an endeavour to read the future.

Now any attempt to read the future must be based on past experience. If, for instance, a certain set of circumstances has given rise in the past to a certain result, then it is logical to assume that when those circumstances recur, the same result will follow. If, then, past results can be traced to their originating circumstances, management need only be able to recognise those circumstances when they occur again in order to be able to predict the result with fair certainty.

This, of course, omits consideration of the unexpected but, in fact, the truly unexpected very seldom happens. When it does happen, its impact on the mind is the more severe because of its rarity and for that reason unexpected events loom large in the memory. Actions and policies based, as they must often be, on the prediction of future events are, however, stultified at conception if they are to be modified always in deference to the possibility of the unexpected.

Management must accept, therefore, that past history is the best possible guide for future forecasts and, secondly, that accurate future forecasts are an essential of successful management. Past history, then, must be analysed and made to reveal every item of information likely to have a bearing on the future activities of the firm, and management will study its charts over as long as possible a past period and will look for trends.

In any well-established, competently run firm, trends, or indications, will be clearly distinguishable in its charts and, an important factor, it will be found that there is always a cause for each upward or downward trend. The difficulty is to assign the right cause to each.

In detail, of course, each management will make its own decisions in terms of the individual firm but there are certain general considerations that apply widely and which will repay discussion here.

In any sales chart, covering a number of years, it will be possible to dissect four different kinds of trend and to assign to each some specific cause. By so dissecting the chart, a clearer and more useful picture is at once presented and the problem of future forecasting is to that extent simplified.

First there will be seen the long-term upward trend, indicative of the gradual growth and expansion of the business. We shall discuss, in Chapter XV, the problems of development so, for the moment, it must be accepted that every business must develop or decline.

The long-term trend will, by its nature, be gradual and there may be many set-backs but, by charting figures at quarterly or yearly intervals, the upward trend of a successful business will be visible and measurable.

Secondly, management will look for the seasonal trend,

indicative of the seasonal rises and falls to which nearly every business is subject, some in summer, others in winter. These peaks and valleys will also be clearly distinguished in a sales chart.

Thirdly, there are the trends that are inseparable from the trade cycles—slumps and booms—that have been a characteristic feature of industry and commerce for many decades.

These cycles will make their mark on the sales charts and can easily be distinguished by careful study.

Finally, circumstances individual to the business will also be recorded in the form of peaks or valleys. It may, for example, be customary for the firm to close down completely for a fortnight in the summer; on the other hand it may be that the firm handles a certain large order regularly at the same time each year. In these and similar cases, the attendant falls and rises on the chart will be clearly distinguishable.

Sorting out and recognising these different trends is one thing ; using the information is quite another and a word or two on the latter will not be out of place.

Remembering that the main object of studying the charts is to recognise trends in advance and to benefit by the fore-knowledge of coming events, we can now see how management should act when confronted with a predicted change in sales levels.

In the case of the long-term trend, management will concern itself with maintaining a gradual upward climb and swiftly stepping in to thwart any downward tendency.

The seasonal trend can often be levelled out to some extent by securing work of a contra-seasonal nature; work, that is, likely to be required in a normally slack period. Wise management can achieve this by offering special inducements to customers and additional rewards to salesmen for such orders of the desired kind as they may secure.

When considering the trade-cycle trends, matters are less in the hands of management than in the hands of national policy but, even so, forewarning of an impending slump can frequently stimulate management to avoid its worst effects and to bring into force necessary economies at the earliest possible time.

The individual trends can be used to measure the actual effect of individual policy. If the firm does shut down for a fortnight, what is the effect in terms of sales figures ? If a large order is handled at regular but infrequent intervals, can other work be found to fill in the less busy months ? Questions like these can be asked by any management but intelligent answers can only come from a close study of the charts.

Before leaving the subject of statistics, three terms in common use should, perhaps, be explained.

Reference is frequently made to a moving average and unless one is reasonably familiar with charts and their uses, confusion may well arise, though, in fact, the calculation of a moving average is simplicity itself ; further, its use in appropriate circumstances is substantial.

To obtain, say, the average monthly sales over a period of a year one would, of course, add together the monthly totals for twelve months and divide the sum by twelve, the quotient being the desired average.

To translate this into a moving average, all that need be done, at monthly intervals, is to add to the total the most recent month's figures and subtract therefrom the least recent, leaving a sum made up of the twelve most recent monthly totals, varying each month as the adjustment is made. Monthly division of the current total by twelve supplies regular monthly moving averages.

The value of the moving average lies in the fact that it evens out any seasonal inequalities and shows the general trend of the figures for comparison with current achievements. By charting the monthly moving average against current monthly figures and against cumulative monthly figures over the year, upward and downward trends become most marked.

Finally, reference is often made to logarithmic and arithmetic scales and, as each has its specific use, the difference must be explained.

The scale on an ordinary sales chart is an arithmetic one, in that each vertical division represents the same value. An inch, for example, might indicate a rise from £1,000 to £2,000 or from £12,000 to £13,000. For a simple sales chart, this is all that is necessary and can cause no confusion.

Imagine, though, a chart comparing sales with net profit, the sales curve being somewhere in the region of £20,000 and the net profit curve at the £2,000 level.

Now, if these curves were plotted on an arithmetic scale, it is easy to see that a rise of £5,000 in both sales and net profit would result in two upward and parallel slanting lines, indicating to the eye a similarity which does not, in fact, exist. On the figures given, net profit would have increased from 10 per cent to 28 per cent of sales—a truly startling event, and one not to be concealed by unsuitable charting.

For comparisons of this nature, then, a logarithmic scale is used, either by acquiring specially ruled paper or by charting the logarithms of the ordinates.

The effect of this is to show increases and decreases in any two or more curves as proportionate to each other. In the case stated, the rise in the net profit curve would be startlingly steep and would indicate at once that a wholly disproportionate change had taken place.

The logarithmic and arithmetic scales both have their place in statistical representation and each should be used according to the nature of the figures to be charted and the purpose of the chart when constructed.

CHAPTER VIII

How Work is Measured

One of the chief reasons for a factory's existence is the production of finished goods to meet the demands of its customers without whom it could not exist.

To produce in accordance with demands, wherever they originate, implies that, at some point early in the carrying out of production, someone must have some idea of what is to be produced in a given time. In other words, a production schedule must be prepared; further, it must be a schedule capable of being carried out.

To prepare a production schedule without having any idea of the amount of work that can be done in any process in a given time would be a classically impossible task. It would be like asking a man how many bricks he could get into a box without telling him the dimensions of the bricks. It follows, then, that work must be measured and reduced to time-elements that can be applied in advance to all proposed operations in the factory. Only thus can a workable production schedule be prepared and only thus, in turn, can the factory produce to any coherent plan.

It may be argued that many small factories to-day are producing happily and efficiently without a production schedule; this is false reasoning. It is true that in many small factories no written schedule is prepared—and they are unwise in this respect—but a schedule exists nevertheless, usually in the mind of the works manager who must know, from his experience, how long any job will take to complete. The weakness of this method is that no works manager is everlasting and he will have to be succeeded some day.

Again, it is almost invariable practice for the customer to ask for an estimate, or for the Board to require a price, before production begins. Without an accurate idea of how long the work will take, no such estimate can be given as time taken and ultimate cost are inseparable from each other. Work, then, must be measured.

The process of measuring work is a thorough one, if properly undertaken, and does not consist merely of measuring work as it is being done at the time ; it includes within it means of ensuring that the work to be measured is being done in the most economical way possible. This means is known as motion study.

You will realise, if you think about it, that any manual operation, however simple or however complex, consists of a connected series of limb and body movements, some lasting only a fraction of a second ; others longer. You will realise, too, that these movements are being made some hundreds or thousands of times a day by every factory worker.

Motion study, therefore, is a technique of which the object is to study these individual movements, finding out whether they are necessary, whether they are being made in the quickest way and whether they are being made in the way least tiring to the operative. By eliminating unnecessary movement and by altering necessary movements to make them quicker and less tiring to perform, motion study, properly applied, can save production time and, concurrently, reduce industrial fatigue.

One's first impression, perhaps, is that it is scarcely worth while to spend money and brain-power on a technique that may reduce a hand-movement from half a second to two-fifths but, when that hand movement is made a thousand times a day or more by possibly several hundred operatives, the significance of motion study will be appreciated. It is a case of getting big results from attention to small beginnings.

Motion study is not a technique to be undertaken by the untrained, though much useful information can be secured by reading some of the literature on the subject, such as the writings of Frank Gilbreth.

Gilbreth was one of the earliest people to realise that all action, whether of hand, foot or body, was capable of being reduced to a limited number of precisely similar fundamental movements. He saw that these movements were present in the actions of pressing a button, picking up and using a screw driver, positioning work on the bench and, in fact, in all activities common to factory production.

By careful research he succeeded in distinguishing and coding all these separate, and sometimes infinitesimal, movements of finger, hand, arm, foot, leg and body. The code symbols he called therbligs.

It was then possible to translate any production operation into therbligs and record it for study and analysis, aiming always, of course, at the elimination of every useless movement which could slow down the operation or increase the fatigue of the performer.

These useless movements arose sometimes from bad habits acquired unconsciously by the operative, sometimes from bad positioning or layout of the work.

Once distinguished and separated from the useful movements, they could, Gilbreth argued, be done away with by proper training in the job and by improving the work layout, altering bench heights and arranging means for easier handling of materials to be processed.

Whether management should, in all cases, go so far into motion study as did Gilbreth is, of course, a matter of production economics. If a certain job is performed a few times a day by only one operative, it would clearly be unnecessary to set up cine-cameras and employ highly-trained motion study experts to analyse it. On the other hand, if a job is performed thousands of times a day in a big factory by hundreds of operatives, considerable sums could well and wisely be spent in reducing the time taken per operation by even a small fraction of a second.

Having taken such steps as are necessary to ensure that each operation performed in the factory is being performed as quickly and as tirelessly as possible, steps can now be taken to measure the work. This is done by setting standard times for the operations which, after the application of motion study, are themselves composed of standard fundamental elements.

Time study, as the measuring process is called, links up closely with motion study but is, nevertheless, something quite different in conception. The object of time study is to ascertain how long any operation should take to perform.

This does not mean that a record is wanted of the fastest possible time, nor does it mean that a record is wanted of the usual time taken. What is wanted is a record of a good, economical target time which will act as an inducement to the slower worker but which can be achieved by all who are competent at their job.

To set as standard the fastest possible time would be to dishearten all those who, however willing, were not record-breakers, while to set an excessively slow time would be to nullify the effects of time study altogether. The aim must be to set a good medium time, making allowance for fatigue and other interrupting factors inherent in any work process.

The simplest way of making a time study is by the use of a stop-watch applied to the work of a normally competent, but not exceptionally quick, operative. This method, however, has its disadvantages.

The use of a stop-watch in a factory has for many years, given rise to grave distrust, originating, possibly, in early attempts, inadequately explained, to apply the benefits of time study. The belief is rife that time study is applied only with the object of driving the operative to work faster and harder for the benefit, solely, of the employer. It is easy to see how this fallacy arose but not so easy to see how to eradicate it.

Time study, as has already been said, is applied with the twofold object of producing more output in less time and of reducing fatigue in the operative. Further, by means of incentives which we discuss in the next chapter, faster work can actually lead to lower cost to the employer and greater reward to the operative.

Education along these lines can do much to overcome stop-watch suspicion but, even so, it will often be found that the operative being timed will work deliberately at an artificial speed, either faster or slower than usual. This makes stop-watch technique largely useless if it cannot be overcome.

If a works council exist, and if co-operation can be secured in the matter of stop-watches, this will probably prove the most effective way of overcoming opposition on the factory floor. This is especially true if a works council delegate accompanies the time study engineer in his work, thereby giving confidence to the operatives.

Sometimes, though, for reasons stated or because of the nature of the job to be timed, the use of a stop-watch is impossible and recourse must be had to other means.

Of these, the most usual is the keeping of actual, and carefully checked, production details over a period of some weeks or months. If from these it is found that the fastest worker performs a certain operation 120 times an hour and the slower worker 85 times in the same period, it will not be difficult to set a time, say 36 seconds or 100 operations per hour, which will be well within the compass of every operative if he cares to exert himself.

Once set, this time becomes the basis on which estimates are prepared and to which standard costs, if used, are related. It is also the target time for the operation and is used in all planning and scheduling of work through the factory. With a standard time for all operations, all these activities are greatly simplified.

To repeat, motion and time study, properly applied, first ensure that each individual operation is being performed as easily and as economically as possible and, secondly, put on record the time each operation should take to perform.

This is all very well, someone may say, but who's going to ensure that the operatives themselves appreciate the economies and efficiencies of all this ? Why should they work harder to achieve a standard time ? Why should they work the way the motion study man tells them when they've been doing the job their own way for years without complaint ? These are good points but the questioner will have to wait until the next chapter for his answer.

Even to-day, after all that has been written about the subject, too scant attention has been paid to the advantages of motion and time study. This is still the prerogative of the large concern and is often held in some contempt by the managers of small businesses. This is a pity and militates against good management since it is the small manufacturer who represents by far the greater part of the production facilities of the country. He must learn that motion and time study is not a luxury and that he can afford it; indeed, all too often he can't afford not to explore this aid to management.

He must rid himself of this muddled thinking—and there must be no more muddled thinking in management than there is magic. The smaller manufacturer who wants to manage his business on modern lines will have to realise that motion and time study, applied economically, must find a place in his management activities.

Finally, to give an idea of what can be achieved by work measurement, the following actual instance, taken from an American source, may be quoted.

The firm concerned carried out, as one of its processes, the boxing of stockings. The operation involved picking up a pair of stockings, wrapping it, placing it in the box, putting the lid on and sticking on a label indicative of the contents.

The girls performing this work had acquired a natural deftness born of long usage and were found to be taking an average of 13.2 seconds for the complete cycle of operations.

Steps were then taken to study the movements and the work layout generally. Waste movements were eliminated, bench fixtures to hold the boxes were fitted and the positions of stockings, wrappers and labels were so altered as to call for a minimum of time and effort in reaching them. In some cases the heights of the stools were altered to reduce fatigue.

A standard method of performing the task was then evolved and all girls trained to adopt it in place of their own self-taught methods.

Within a remarkably short space of time—weeks rather than months—the girls were working at full speed in the new way and were performing the task in 5.8 seconds instead of 13.2 seconds.

The cost of carrying out the motion and time studies, making all the necessary adjustments and training the girls in the new methods was just over £600.

On the face of it, perhaps, spending £600 to save 7.4 seconds per girl per operation may seem uneconomic; many firms would think so, anyway. This is short sighted.

Suppose that the girls were earning 4s. 6d. (22½p) per hour each. Under the old methods, each complete boxing operation would carry a wage cost of .198d (.0825p) while, under the new conditions, the wage cost would be .087d. (.03625p) —a saving of .111d. (.04625p) on each box of stockings.

One girl, working full time under the new conditions, would be completing 620 boxing operations an hour or, say, a million and a quarter in a year of 2,000 working hours—and a million and a quarter times .111d. (.04625p) is nearly £579. It is this figure that must be taken into account when deciding whether or not the project is worth while financially.

In fact, the cost would be recovered even more quickly since the computation takes no account of consequential saving in overhead expenses.

Put this way, it may well be agreed that few manufacturers can afford not to spend £400 in order to reduce the wage costs on one repetitive item by over 50 per cent and that work measurement is a vital concomitant to good management.

CHAPTER IX

How Incentives are Applied

In the last chapter, the argument was made for work-measurement. It was shown not only that work could be measured but also that it must be measured if estimating is not to remain guesswork, if production planning is not to become impossible and if, in short, management is to keep any control at all over the productive processes of the factory.

It was seen that every operation must become the subject of a standard time within which it should be completed and on which all calculations would be based. We are now to consider how the operatives themselves are to be induced to work to the standard time or, if possible, even faster, though, to preserve the purpose of the standard time, no operative will be expected to exceed it by any substantial extent. Indeed, if the time be properly set, no operative will be able to exceed it very substantially.

The inducement to the operative is the incentive which, in short, means that the faster and more accurate worker receives, in proportion, a heavier wage packet than his slower and less accurate colleagues. This, after all, is only fair in principle but, before elaborating on how a just result is achieved, two matters must be cleared up.

First, I am using the word " incentive " in the limited sense of financial incentive and, in so doing, excluding for the moment other inducements of a non-financial nature that are often offered with the same object. To these I shall refer later.

Secondly, much muddled thinking has been devoted to the economics of incentives and many people have come to believe that, in effect, they tend to increase cost. If, it is argued, a man be paid more for working harder, the price per article must surely be increased. This is not so.

We have already seen, in Chapter VI, that the cost of an article comprises raw material, wages and overhead expenses, these last two being directly related to the time taken in production. If then, that time be reduced, both the wage and the overhead expense element will be reduced with it, the cost being reduced accordingly.

The aim of good management, therefore, is so to scale the incentive payments that they provide the maximum inducement to the operative and yet do not exceed the amount by which the cost is reduced because of greater speed of production.

In attempts to find this optimum level for various industries, a great many formulæ have been devised. Most of these have served their purpose in the limited sphere for which they were created but, so diverse are the needs of industry, it is impossible to say that any system of incentives yet devised is the ideal for any industry. A few of the more usual systems must, then, be described with the reminder that adaptations of these—or even entirely different formulæ —may be equally effective in certain circumstances.

The simplest form of incentive is the piece-rate system, in which a price is set by the rate-fixer, acting on behalf of the management, for every series of operations resulting in a measurable unit of the product. At the end of the day, or week, the number of units produced is totalled, rejected output being discounted, and multiplied by the price per unit. The result is what the operative receives as wages. Thus, the more the operative produces, the more he gets and the price is so fixed that by working full factory hours at the standard time he gets rather more than he would by working on a weekly wage, or time rate.

The disadvantage of this system is that no accurate time records are kept as they are not necessary, and, unless specifically demanded, much information of great use is lost to management. Further, since the operative is only paid for what he actually produces, there is a tendency for him to take time off or keep irregular hours whenever he feels inclined and management has very little power to correct him. Production thus may become erratic and much of the value of work-measurement may be lost.

For these reasons, and others peculiar to individual industries, a custom has come into being by means of which the operative's pay is made up of two elements. First, he gets paid at a standard rate for all the time he spends on the factory and is available for work; secondly, he is given an incentive bonus directly related to the extent by which he exceeds the standard output which he is expected to achieve. Two systems of this type will be sufficiently characteristic of the methods used, of which there is an almost infinite variety.

The first incentive-bonus system to be described is that known as the Halsey-Weir and its object is to share fairly between management and operative the wage-saving resulting from faster work on the part of the latter.

As a preliminary, the work to be done will have been measured and rates will have been set, the result being converted into a set task of so many units per hour. This is the standard task.

If the operative performs the standard task he receives only his hourly time rate, calculated from his weekly wage. The same applies if he performs less than the standard task.

If, on the other hand, the operative exceeds the standard task by completing it in less than the time set, he receives, in addition to his hourly time rate, a bonus equal to one-third of the value of the time he has saved, calculated in terms of his own wages. This may be a little confusing but the example will clear it up.

Let us suppose that a man earning 15s. 0d. (75p) per hour is set a task for which the standard time is eight hours. If he completes the work in nine hours, he receives nine times 15s. 0d. (75p) or 135s. 0d. (£6.75).

If he completes the task in eight hours, he receives eight times 15s. 0d. (75p) or 120s. 0d. (£6). Neither of these payments include any bonus element as he has not exceeded his target output.

Now suppose that, by working more diligently, he completes the task in seven hours. He then receives seven times 15s. 0d. (75p), or 105s. 0d. (£5.25), and, because he has exceeded his target output, he gets a bonus of one-third of the hour he has saved in terms of his hourly rate or one-third of 15s. 0d. (75p) which is 5s. 0d. (25p). For his seven hours' work, therefore, he receives 105s. 0d. (£5.25) plus 5s. 0d. (25p) or 110s. 0d. (£5.50). This, for seven hours' work, is equal to just over 15s. 8d. (78½p) per hour.

This system is simple to calculate and its incentive force is adjustable by varying arbitrarily the one-third ratio. On the other hand, if the task be badly set, strange results may occur and it sometimes happens, especially in new work, that tasks are badly set.

Suppose, to see what happens, that this operative finds it possible to complete the task in one hour instead of the standard eight. His receipts will be 15s. 0d. (75p) for the hour worked plus a bonus of one-third of seven hours saved at 15s. 0d. (75p) per hour, or 35s. 0d. (£1.75). His hourly wage is thus 50s. 0d. (£2.50).

It was to counter this possibility that the Rowan system was devised. This is rather more complicated to work out but has the merit that, however badly the task is set, no operative can ever earn double time rate or more.

The Rowan formula calculates first the percentage of time saved to standard time set and then applies this percentage to the money earned or time rate. Again, an example.

Assume, as before, that the hourly time rate is 15s. 0d. (75p) and the task is eight hours. As in the Halsey-Weir system, an operative taking standard time or longer only gets his 15s. 0d. (75p) per hour.

If, though, he completes the work in seven hours, he receives seven times 15s. 0d (75p)—105s. 0d. (£5.25)—plus 12½ per cent (one-eighth saving on time allowed) of 105s. 0d (£5.25), making a total payment for the seven hours of 118s. 1d. (£5.90½). This represents an hourly rate of just over 16s. 10d. (84p). This is rather higher than the rate he would have received under the Halsey-Weir system.

If, on the other hand, we take the extreme case of the man who completes a set eight-hour task in one hour, and apply the Rowan formula to it, the advantages of this system to the employer will be obvious. The operative will, in these circumstances, receive 15s. 0d. (75p) for the hour he works plus 87½ per cent (seven-eighths saving on time allowed) of 15s. 0d. (75p) or 13s. 2d. (66p), making a total of 28s. 2d. (£1.41) for one hour's work.

Some may feel that devising special systems to cope with possible mistakes in the setting of tasks is unnecessary since, if the task be wrongly set, the time can be adjusted as soon as this becomes apparent. Unfortunately, this is just what can't be done.

Once set and agreed, times must not be changed unless some material working condition is also changed. To cut rates is the surest possible way of destroying confidence between management and workers; once destroyed, it will be almost impossible to restore it. It behoves management, then, to set rates with all possible care and, if a mistake be made, to carry the penalty.

I must repeat that the piece-rate and the two premium bonus schemes described are only three of an almost infinite variety of ways in which the individual can be rewarded in direct proportion to increased output. Other schemes work on a group basis.

Among the group schemes, too, there is a wide choice varying from the co-partnership agreements to the simple group incentive, applied either to the personnel as a whole or to the small working group.

Under co-partnership, an attempt is made by various legal means to give the workers a share in the prosperity of their company, thereby encouraging them to give of their best.

Some schemes of this nature have worked with notable success but they are not lightly to be undertaken as there are certain inherent drawbacks which require careful consideration if they are to be avoided.

Among these is the fact that, while employees are willing to share profits, they are not willing to share losses. As every company must, at times, expect to meet a bad period, this can lead to grave difficulty.

Again, if employees are to share profits, it is only right that they should have access to the company's accounts, or, at least, to an audited extract therefrom. It is not always easy to devise methods by which the employees can be given the information to which they are entitled without disclosing matters which are usually confidential to the Board Room. These difficulties can be, and often have been, overcome, but they must be foreseen well in advance of the introduction of any form of profit sharing on a co-partnership basis.

The most usual group bonus scheme, applied to the whole factory, takes as a starting point a standard level of production. This may be the average for a certain number of preceding years or may be calculated in relation to a standard costing system. It must, further, be expressed in measurable units, such as production-man-hours or some similar factor common to all kinds of output.

Once set, this standard level becomes the target for the ensuing year and the management undertake to increase all wages or salaries by the percentage by which the target is exceeded. Thus, if the target is exceeded by 10 per cent, a bonus is awarded equal to 10 per cent of each employee's remuneration for the year.

This scheme, and others like it, have the grave disadvantage that the receipt of the bonus by the employee must be delayed until the year's output is completed and assessed. By this time, fifteen months or more may have elapsed since the earliest date on which bonus was earned. This has the effect of divorcing hard work from reward in the employees' minds and undermining the very purpose for which the bonus is paid.

A further difficulty arising with group schemes of this kind is that of dealing with persons who join or leave the company during the year. This, like other disadvantages, can usually be overcome but an equitable arrangement cannot always be found.

The group bonus applied to the small group is much

simpler and more satisfactory. In essence, it may take the form of the individual piece-rate or premium bonus systems already described, but, instead of being calculated in terms of one employee, it is calculated in terms of a group of employees all working as a team on one measurable unit of output, such as an assembly that may pass through five or six hands before completion. In such cases a group scheme may be the only one feasible.

So much for financial incentives; I said earlier in this chapter that they were not the only way in which operatives could be induced to work harder. I now go further and say that they are not even the best way.

In any financial incentive scheme, there cannot but be an element of bribery since every employee is paid a basic wage in return for which he is expected to devote his best energies to the work of his employer. An incentive payment is, by this token, an additional payment for working hard, and contains within it the implication that he needs extra reward for doing what he has already contracted to do for his basic wage.

For this reason, other forms of encouragement and reward are often sought and tried, usually with excellent results.

These non-financial incentives may consist of extra time off, superior status indicated by badges, the award of Challenge Shields to competing units within the factory or, on occasion, even the award of additional paid holidays for the employees showing the best output return of the week.

Like all incentives, there are disadvantages, too, in non-financial incentives, the chief being the possibility of favouritism, open or concealed. It is true that such incentives can be related to measured work but, in practice, they are used more often where the work is of such a nature that measurement is difficult. It then devolves on the overseer or chargehand to nominate the recipients. This is not to say that overseers or chargehands are more susceptible to favouritism than others ; my point is that the award must depend on the individual choice of one man or woman, whatever failings he or she may have.

Awards of this nature can sometimes be made on the advice of the works council and where this is possible much better results can be expected.

Even where no direct incentive is possible—and I have in mind now the craft industries and most offices where the work is not measurable—some incentive must be given; the most usual way is the granting of what are known as merit rises.

These merit rises, or pay increases, mark the recognition by the management of better, faster or generally superior work on the part of the employee. They are not to be confused with the pay increases which recognise greater responsibility and authority.

Sometimes merit rises are given as a result of careful study of the employees' work; at others actual output records are kept over an extended period for it must be remembered, a merit rise once given cannot be taken away.

Salary rises given to mark increased responsibilities fall into quite a different category. The reason for their award is visible to everyone since the recipient will have been promoted or given extra duties to perform and his status will have improved. Good management will, however, take great care that rises of this sort shall be reserved scrupulously for people so promoted. There is a tendency in badly managed organisations to abuse the responsibility-rise system and increase, by means of it, the wages of those who have not been promoted but whom the management want to reward for some quite different reason. This procedure is bound to cast doubts on the whole wage structure and will, inevitably, bring about real and imagined injustices which may well eat away at the very foundations of good staff-relations.

In a small office or factory the rises are usually authorised by one individual who, for that reason, can exercise his sense of justice; in a large organisation the rises are often recommended by many department heads to a management which has little personal knowledge of each nominee's qualities or responsibility.

To obviate such complaints of injustice, wise management will set up a salary grading scale, grouping under eight or ten headings the various levels of responsibility held by employees.

The first group will include those such as secretaries to directors, who carry considerable responsibility, must use a great deal of initiative and in whose hands much of the successful routine of the firm must lie.

At the other end of the scale, the last grade will include office messengers and others who carry a minimum of responsibility and whose activities are entirely directed by others.

Within these extremes, the other grades are defined in declining order of responsibility.

Employees will then be graded according to the jobs they are doing, and allocated to one or other of the groups.

It only remains now to set top and bottom salary levels for each grade, the top level of each overlapping by a small amount the lower level of the grade more senior. The first, or highest grade, has no top salary level.

The scale is then made public and each employee is told his or her grading. They are also told that merit rises within each grade can be awarded for good work by the head of the department without sanction from top management; this materially assists discipline and enhances the status of department heads.

Transfer from one grade to another, however, can only be made by top management after reviewing any cases of changed responsibilities; this keeps the main control in its rightful place.

If properly and equitably done—and this is no light task—nearly all internal jealousy and suspicion can be obviated. Each employee will know that those of equal responsibility are receiving comparable salaries; he will know that he can receive salary increases for good work and, by reference to the grading scale, he can see what position he must achieve if he is to transfer to a higher grade.

If management are still unsure that any possibility of

favouritism or bias is eliminated, they may combine a salary grading scheme with a merit-rating scheme.

For this purpose a form is prepared listing some ten or a dozen qualities desirable in an employee. Punctuality, initiative, capability, influence on fellows, ability to take responsbility and similar qualities are used.

A form for each employee is issued to the head of each department, quarterly or half-yearly, this individual being required to indicate his opinion of his employees by marking each question out of a possible five. Thus, the man frequently late would get one for punctuality while he who was always punctual would get five.

The forms are returned to the personnel manager or director acting in that capacity, and the marks transferred to a register which, in a short while, becomes a good record of every employee's worth. By using it for reference in all applications for up-grading almost complete impartiality is assured.

CHAPTER X

Making the Office Efficient—1

Any business, as we have seen, is conducted by the management with the aid of the five major functions. Management, as it were, uses these functions to achieve its ends rather as the brain uses the limbs. A brain, however, would have little or no control over the limbs were it not for the nerve centres which, briefly, convert the brain's demands into positive action by the limbs. To the extent that the nerve centres are inefficient, so will the liaison between brain and limbs be constricted.

So it is with management, the office playing the part of the nerve centres. If the office be inefficient the best laid plans of higher management must be stultified by inefficient transmission of its requirements to the functional departments who must bring those requirements to fruition.

This applies not only to higher management; it applies all down the scale. Each functional chief is, as we have seen, partly a manager and each, in a large firm especially, will have his own office through which to transmit his instructions.

Thus, if we can indulge in a flight of fancy, we have a picture of higher management passing its instructions on policy and general procedure through a main office where these instructions are broken down into their constituent parts, each concerning one or other of the functions.

These functional instructions are then passed out of the main office to the functional chiefs and the same process is repeated on a smaller scale, the instructions being again passed by way of the functional or departmental office to the actual persons who are to carry out the work.

But that is only half the story.

It will be remembered that mention has been made of the

need for a two-way flow of information, outward from higher management to the functional chiefs and inwards from the functional chiefs to higher management. The outward information consists of the instructions which the managing director gives in order to achieve the Board's policy, the inward information consists of reports and statements on the progress being made and on the extent to which the policy is being carried out. It is on this latter, the inward information, that the managing director relies for his reports to the Board.

So the office, to use the term generically, wherever it be found, is a vital link in the management chain. To the extent to which that link is weak, so can the efficiency of the whole organisation be impaired.

To appreciate this, think of a brilliant managing director, an active and progressive Board, versatile plant, adequate buildings, competent executives, conscientious overseers and capable workers. Put them together and contemplate the result.

Clearly this would be little short of chaos, for the one good reason that the organisation would lack the necessary nerve centres and the brain could not control the limbs. The office, then, must exist and must be efficient.

I make this point at some length because there is, in many quarters, a tendency to decry the office as a centre of " paper-work " and as the source from which emanates a variety of requests for detail, instructions and, sometimes, criticisms. To the man on the job, the actual producer, this all seems unnecessary. He argues that the organisation exists to produce, that he is producing and that any factor tending to take his mind off production must, for that reason, be contrary to the main purpose of the business.

It is true that, all too often, the office does exert a hampering influence on production—but that is due to inefficient office administration ; it is not an argument that the office, as such, is a useless excrescence on the body productive.

As is the case with the functions of management, it is both incorrect and unwise to say that any one of the many activities of the office is more important than any other, though some of these activities do seem more obvious to the casual observer. If asked, for instance, to state briefly the purpose of the office in industry, one might well reply that the office existed for the purpose of communication and record keeping. This, though far from being the whole story, will serve as a starting point for our examination of the office and the means whereby efficiency can be secured.

I shall refer frequently in this and the next chapter to the office manager and I think I should make it clear that, by this designation, I mean either a full-time office manager such as one might find in a large business or a functional executive who, by virtue of his position, is in charge of a departmental office.

I have already pictured the office, wherever it be situated, as the two-way transmitter of information ; in this capacity there is no room for slipshod methods.

The office manager will see to it that a well-understood system is in being whereby all his staff know what information to expect, when and whence to expect it, what to do with it and whither to transmit it.

In some small firms this routine may be so simple that no elaborate plan need be laid down.

In a larger concern, however, and in a great many of the smaller ones, the preparation and publication of a route chart is almost an essential.

A route chart illustrates semi-pictorially the route of every standard or routine document passing through the organisation, showing where each originates, its purpose, its use and its final destination. Since any well-managed firm will have standardised its documentation as far as possible, a chart of this nature will cater for the vast majority of the documents.

The preparation of a route chart is not a difficult matter though it calls for some serious thinking on the part of the office manager.

He will first collect specimens of all the standard documents in use. By these I mean the forms, reports, returns and schedules that are prepared at regular intervals for the use of managers, foremen, supervisors and clerks.

He will then allot them distinguishing numbers or titles and mark the route of each on a suitably prepared plan of the organisation, indicating clearly the point of origin and ultimate destination.

That done, he will consider carefully the routes shown, noting on the plan the purpose for which the document is used by every person through whose hands it passes.

He may well find, if the documentation has not been recently overhauled, that one or more documents are superfluous or that the routes of some are unnecessarily complicated.

He may find that the purpose of one document ceased to exist some time ago ; that by adding to the information on one document and circulating it rather more widely, another can be abolished ; that the route of one document is longer than it need be as it is routed through the hands of people who have no need of the information it contains. By removing these inefficiencies, the whole communication system within the organisation can be streamlined and the manager has the satisfaction of knowing that every document handled in his office has a set purpose and that no time is being wasted on dealing with useless items.

By displaying the route chart and annotating it with, where applicable, dates when information is required at various centres, his staff will be provided with an effective time-table which will tell them not only when and where to communicate information but also where to go for it if it does not come to hand when it should.

Having established a recognised and fully efficient means of routing information the office manager will next turn his attention to record keeping.

This does not mean that he will keep innumerable carbon copies of everything, but it does mean that he will devise means of having at his finger tips all the information that he is likely to need at any time.

How he does this will, of course, depend on the sort of information it is. It may be such as can be charted, it may require tabulated reports or ledgers or it may be the sort that can be kept in filing cabinets. Whatever it is, its whole force lies in its availability—information that is not available when it is wanted is valueless.

The route chart and the record keeping will, naturally, be closely allied with the office organisation itself. Here the ordinary rules of organisation apply.

The office manager will certainly see that his staff is the best he can get and he will try to select people of an intelligence level matched to the kind of jobs they will have to do. Few situations are more demoralising than those in which a highly intelligent and ambitious clerk is set to perform, day after day, some task so simple as to make no demands on his thinking power. To allow such situations to arise is bad for the staff, bad for the business and, as a corollary, bad office management.

Having done his best to suit temperament and abilities to jobs, the office manager's next concern will be to see that everyone knows what to do, how to do it and when to do it. He will spend as long as may be necessary on this as he will know that once a clerk has been instructed he must be left alone to do the job. He must not be subjected to constant badgering and interference from above.

Each clerk will be told the extent of his responsibility and, of course, given authority commensurate with it. It is useless to make a clerk responsible for preparing a schedule once a week unless, at the same time, he be given authority to call for, and demand if necessary, the information he needs for the purpose. However small the responsibility or however great, authority must match it.

The same thing applies in reverse, of course. No doubt many will have had experience of the man, sometimes the relation of a director, given an indeterminate job of little responsibility to keep him occupied. Possessing a large measure of authority derived by proxy, as it were, from his connection with the Board, such a man can, and often does, create havoc in the office before the rot is stopped. In the words of the textbook, " Responsibility and authority must at all times be co-equal, co-extensive and co-determinate."

The office manager will be always mindful that his office is not an entity in itself. It is part of an organisation and must recognise the existence of other offices and departments. Recognition, in this sense, means that each office or department must co-operate to co-ordinate the work flowing through.

It is more important, far more important, to achieve a smooth flow of information and inter-communication than it is to bicker and eventually prove that a vital hold-up originated somewhere else. Some office managers seem to think otherwise, to their detriment, and are more interested in winning an inter-departmental wrangle than they are in seeing that their office does the task set it in full co-operation with others.

I have already said that the mental ability and development of individual members of the staff must be related to the duties allotted them. These duties, in brief, will range from supervising the franking machine, fetching and carrying and getting tea at one end of the scale to, at the other end, duties usual to a confidential secretary who may, in the absence of the office manager, be called upon to take quite important decisions. Between these extremes will lie that host of clerical duties which includes book-keeping, shorthand-typing, filing, calculating, telephone operating and the like.

The problem of the office manager is to match all these jobs with clerks mentally attuned to them. This is not an easy task, nor is it possible, in every case, to succeed. If, however, the office manager is a skilful handler of personnel and if he has a natural sympathy with people less fortunately placed than himself, he will construct a happy community in which it will be a pleasure to work. If he can achieve this, then he can go further and embark on a system of rotation of duties.

This does not mean that, from time to time, the manager's secretary makes the tea while the office boy struggles with her typewriter and filing equipment but it does mean that a periodic change round of like duties is arranged. The advantages are great though the initial problems are not to be discounted.

By alternating the work of, say, three clerks of approximately equal ability, each is given an added interest in his job. Instead of slaving away at a monotonous task, of which he sees neither beginning nor end, each knows that at approximately three- or six-monthly intervals he will have a change of work. By seeing beyond the fringe of his usual work, he can, in addition, get it in perspective.

The office manager will, of course, be closely watching the effects of this duty rotation and, of his wisdom, will quickly be able to select for promotion those clerks who possess any special aptitude or who show exceptional versatility. He will, incidentally, promote the worthy ones as soon as appropriate even if this means their transfer from his office. To hold on to a youngster ripe for promotion just because it is inconvenient to spare him is the best way of guaranteeing a disgruntled and frustrated staff.

Perhaps the supreme advantage of duty rotation lies in the benefits it affords at times of holidays and sickness. Instead of frantic *ad hoc* improvisations, borrowings of untrained clerks from other departments and the overloading of a few willing workers, the fact that all the staff are versatile and used to each other's work makes the whole process simple.

I have taken for my example three clerks of nearly equal ability. In a large office, given careful thought, the process can be expanded to include almost the whole staff, even the office manager himself rotating more routine duties with his deputy.

Before passing on to discuss methods, systems and forms, I would like to say something of—and to—the office manager himself.

He should be a student of management and a humanitarian, seeing his staff as a group of individuals, not as a soulless body of people paid to serve the interests of the company.

The office manager will see to it that he knows precisely

what the job of his office is, where it begins and where it ends. He will also have a very fair understanding of what his colleagues are doing and how their various duties link up with his own. He will be always on the alert to devise means of increasing the service which his office can render to the business.

There is much more I could say to the office manager but, as most of it is dealt with elsewhere in this book, I will confine myself to one more piece of advice.

The office manager must always make sure that all his activities are known to and understood by his deputy. He should regard this individual as in training for his own job in due course. Point will be given to this by an example.

An office manager had been in the same job for almost more years than he could remember. Newcomers had joined the firm, achieved promotion and passed him by on the ladder but still he stuck at the same desk.

He did his work excellently, was relied on by all, and, when he was away sick or on holiday, his department almost collapsed without his presence.

It was not till he came to retirement age that the management of the firm disclosed that they simply could not have promoted him since he was the only one who knew the job. He had kept all his activities, his files and his records private and had so discouraged any attempt by others to learn his job that at no time had there been anyone to take his place.

Of course, the higher management was at fault in some respects but the moral of my story is this. That office manager was so scared of letting anyone else know how the job was done, for fear, presumably, of rendering himself redundant, that he had made his own promotion impossible. There is a lesson here for many office managers who may be tempted to pride themselves on being indispensable.

In addition to having the right man in charge, another factor of importance to the efficiency of the office is the office method in use. By method I mean the routine procedure, the system of internal communication and, of course, the inevitable forms.

As there are as many methods, systems and forms in use as there are offices, any worth-while description would be impossible. Further, the devising of methods and systems and the design of forms are not, by definition, a part of management. It falls within the technical, not the managerial, part of the office manager's job. Even so, it will do no harm to mention a few considerations that should govern the introduction of any new methods, systems or forms.

Broadly, the details of the methods and systems will depend on the kind of work being done by the office as a unit. One would not expect, for example, to find the same methods and systems in use in a works office and an accounts department. On the other hand, certain fundamentals apply to all.

To be effective and efficient, a system must be smooth working; for this reason it should be subjected at regular intervals to an overhaul by the office manager. He should apply a technique similar to that described for the routing of forms, examining the system in all its aspects and asking himself whether some improvement can be made.

The same applies to the methods by which the system is carried out. Far too many methods are perpetuated simply because they have been used for more years than anyone can remember. This is no criterion at all of good methods. Any number of intra-departmental changes may have taken place and it is quite likely that the methods in use may be hopelessly out of date. A regular overhaul will serve to show this and to make possible the discontinuation of any method which may long ago have lost its usefulness.

Designing forms, I find, is sometimes left to haphazard chance, no attempt being made to standardise or regularise the forms in use. This is a pity and militates against efficiency.

True, an individual office manager may not be in a position to revise the design of all forms in use in his company. He can, though, use his influence to get his colleagues' agreement to a general re-designing so that, when done, all forms in use look like members of one family.

Standardisation of design can be carried to quite far

limits irrespective of the nature of the form or its purpose. Standard sizes can be used, thus simplifying ultimate filing, standard positions can be used for such items as form number, job number, customer's name and address, cash values and the like.

Further, the use of the forms can be simplified and possibilities of misuse reduced by printing on each form its route and destination. Different-coloured paper can be used to show point of origin or destination and each form can carry in small type a note of the way in which it is to be filled in and routed. All this is particularly useful when new employees are called on to deal with a system already in being.

A further simplification of working can be achieved by arranging to have a reference number printed on each form. This reference number, appearing in very small type in the bottom left-hand corner can consist of an index letter, indicating the department responsible for re-ordering and a serial number applicable to each different form.

By using these reference numbers when re-ordering from the printer and internally when drawing from stock, all possibility of confusion can be abolished.

All forms should be well printed and carry space for the initials of the person responsible for their accuracy. The reason for this lies in the fact that people will unconsciously take more care over an entry if the form itself is clear, carefully drawn up and well printed and if, by their signature or initials, they know that any mistake can be traced back.

Before leaving this matter of forms, I would add that, where appropriate, forms should be issued made up into tear-off pads, thereby eliminating a possible source of waste.

In my next chapter I propose to deal with the internal layout and administration of the office in more specific detail but, before doing so, I feel I should say something about mechanical office aids.

These include the typewriter, the telephone, adding and calculating equipment, dictating machines and, increasingly as time passes, complete punched-card accounting systems. In very large offices, electronic computers are now used for a variety of tasks that could not, before their introduction, be carried out economically by the human mind. These, however, are hardly within the scope of this book since they must be serviced by technical specialists. It is the job of the office manager, though, to acquaint himself with their capabilities. Even if we exclude computers, we are still left with a number of mechanical office aids which the office manager must employ as the tools of his trade.

Any good craftsman uses tools appropriate to the task in hand. He does not use a sledge-hammer to drive in a tack; the office manager will be guided by the same consideration.

All mechanical office equipment is invaluable when it is fittingly used. Most office jobs can be assisted by mechanisation and a great deal of time can be saved by sensible mechanisation but it does not follow that mechanisation of the office is an end in itself.

Every office manager should, as part of the development side of his job, consider from time to time the merit of mechanising this or that operation. He will not need to be a cost accountant to weigh up the economics of each case.

It is largely a matter of assessing the amount of time mechanisation would save and the value of the time saved in relation to the cost of mechanisation. There may also be intervening factors which cannot be ignored, such as shortage of staff, pressure of work, limitations of space and possible expansion of the services of the office. These will probably defeat any attempt to value them in terms of cash but each will be weighed carefully before a decision is reached and the merits of each assessed impartially.

Finally, with all the mechanical office aids at his disposal, no office manager will be successful unless he gives prime consideration to his staff as individuals. They are the people without whom all office aids are merely complex pieces of metal and machinery—useless unless manipulated intelligently and willingly by men and women, each of whom is an individual with ambitions, sympathies and antipathies, all of which must be given due consideration by the office manager.

With this subject I finish my generalisations on an efficient office and, I believe, leave the way clear for the more detailed survey which follows.

CHAPTER XI

Making the Office Efficient—2

In the preceding chapter I compared the various departmental offices with the nerve centres of the body and implied
that no nerve centre can be expected to work well and do its
job if it be constricted ; the same applies to offices. It is
useless to require miracles of efficiency to be performed
continuously unless the members of the office staff have
room to do their work comfortably and move around freely
on their lawful occasions.

No hard and fast rule can be laid down regarding the
amount of space to be allowed per clerical worker but the
Offices, Shops and Railway Premises Act, 1963 lays down
certain guiding principles. Broadly speaking, this brings
offices, shops and railway premises within the restrictions of
and subject to the provisions of the Factories Acts which
have controlled industrial conditions—in terms of health,
safety and welfare—for many decades past.

As regards situation, an ideal can be stated but seldom
achieved. Clearly the office should be as centrally placed
as possible within the activities—or limbs—of which it is in
control. To depart from this precept is to lengthen the lines
of communication, call for more telephonic, and less personal,
contact, slow down the flow and interchange of information,
and, to that collective extent, to impair efficiency.

There is no need for the office to be lavishly furnished,
though a case can be made out for a certain amount of luxury
in the case of a sales office. It is probable, in these days,
however, that a customer will buy where he finds the best
quality and service rather than where he can most comfortably
relax. Managerial dignity, to be discussed later, also supports
a case for the rather more luxurious furnishing of the private

offices of senior executives. These sanctums, however, do not fall within the terms of reference of this chapter.

It is important, when considering the furnishing of offices, to pay considerable regard to standardisation. Not only do standard office fittings give, of themselves, an air of efficiency, they assist materially in the smooth and simple conduct of office routine.

Particularly is this so in the case of filing systems, but it also applies in the case of chairs, desks, typewriters and other office appliances, when there is in operation a staff-rotation scheme such as was described in the preceding chapter.

The layout of the office is another matter to which thoughtful attention must be given. It is not sufficient to arrange the desks in some sort of order, fill in odd spaces with filing cabinets and leave it at that.

The work should flow through the office in as orderly manner as can be achieved and this aim is best served by arranging for the various clerks to sit in the order in which they handle the work flow. If this be neglected, a situation will develop in which each clerk is repeatedly getting up and crossing the office to collect or deliver documents, files and the like. In itself this is a bad thing but add to it the loss of time occupied by the clerks in the inevitable short conversation that attends a visit to another desk and the inefficiencies due to bad layout can be seen in full.

The office having been laid out in the way best calculated to secure a smooth flow of work, lighting, ventilation and telephones can receive attention, the aim, of course, being to give each clerk adequate—and preferably independent—lighting, to keep the office at an equable temperature without draughts and to provide, for all appropriate clerks, telephones so situated that they can use them without leaving their desks and without straining and stretching. These things can all be done with a little thought, and to the possible remark that I am harping on the obvious, I would reply that that little obvious thought is all too seldom given.

A harmonious office is in a fair way to becoming an efficient office and, since salaries are the most frequent cause of disharmony, the office manager will turn his attention to these at the earliest moment possible.

There are, broadly speaking, two methods by which salaries can be assessed, the impromptu and the scientific, the former being by far the more widely used.

The impromptu method of assessing salaries attempts to reconcile in the case of each individual clerk the salary the clerk would like, what the firm can afford to pay, the value of the work done by the clerk and the salary levels being earned by other clerks. It is not surprising that attempts to reconcile these irreconcilables are seldom wholly successful. This is far from being a satisfactory method based, as it is, on a wide variety of imponderables. It may work moderately well in a small office where each individual and his or her work are known to the office manager but it is always liable to break down when the state of the employment market is such that newcomers are demanding higher salaries than those of comparable, long service employees.

The scientific method of salary grading is based primarily on the economic value of each employee to the firm, assessing that value in terms of responsibility. Once started, it is simple and just as between one clerk and another and it contains within it provision for adjustment in accordance with outside influences, such as the cost of living.

The most difficult part is the initial establishment of the grades and a great deal of care must be taken in defining these in such a way that each grade is clearly and obviously distinct from the others.

Nearly all office work—and nearly all employees in offices —can be grouped, in terms of responsibility, into six or eight grades, as was described in Chapter IX. The top grade applies to directors' secretaries and others with maximum responsibility at office level while the bottom grade applies to office juniors, messengers and the like whose every activity is ordered by someone senior. Within these extremes, the intervening steps are set up and defined.

Each grade is now allotted a top and bottom salary level based on what the firm can afford in relation to the salaries paid for similar work by competitors. The lower level salaries should be sufficient to attract newcomers while the higher level for each grade should represent generous treatment such as would be accorded to a valued long-service employee. No top salary level is set for the top grade so that there is, in effect, no ceiling to the scale.

Each employee and his work are now considered individually and carefully and allotted to the appropriate grade, a list of all of which is made public to all employees.

It is also made known that every employee will be paid a salary not less than the minimum for his grade and that increases for good work can be given by the office manager at regular intervals until the employee is earning the maximum for his grade. He must then apply to higher management for re-grading.

In examining his case, account will be taken of the work he is doing, the work he is capable of doing and of vacancies in the next higher category of work. In the event that the employee cannot be up-graded, he is told so and no objection is raised should he wish to leave.

This last condition is an important one in the smooth working of the scheme but it is often held to be impracticable, as it might result in the firm losing the services of valuable employees. This is true, but as the only alternative is the retention of those employees in a frustrated and disgruntled humour, it is probably better to lose a few in the interests of harmony and loyalty among the remainder.

When a salary grading scale is in being, of course, all newcomers are offered starting salaries within the appropriate grade and the whole scheme is explained to them so that their steps of promotion are made clear, as also are the responsibilities for which they must qualify themselves in order to deserve promotion.

When a vacancy occurs, the procedure is for the manager of the office concerned to notify the personnel manager, or other official charged with finding recruits, that a vacancy exists in such and such a grade and that he requires a male or female clerk to fill it.

In due course, after advertisement or contact with sources of supply, applicants present themselves for interview, first by the personnel manager who prepares a short list of those whom he deems suitable.

The short list is then sent to the manager of the office where the vacancy exists and, after further interview, the final selection is made.

Appointing an applicant to fill a vacancy should not, by a long way, be the end of the matter; though, in a great many firms, from this point the newcomer is left to sink or swim without further help or guidance from anyone. This is a wasteful process and waste cannot find place in an efficient office.

Clearly, a trained employee is worth much more to the firm than one untrained and the office manager must make himself responsible for seeing that every newcomer undergoes some measure of training starting on the first day at work and continuing throughout his time in the office.

It is not suggested that a scholastic atmosphere pervade the office but it is suggested that, at all stages in the career of each employee, some senior shall be directly responsible for his progressive development. This is merely the practical application of the doctrine that every man does three jobs— the job he is paid to do, learning to do the next senior job and, thirdly, teaching someone to succeed him when the time comes for promotion.

In a matter of promotion, the grading scale will be the guiding factor, as has already been explained. Merit rises within the individual grades will be given by the office manager in recognition of good work; upgrading in recognition of increased responsibility will be granted on the sanction of higher management who will, thereby, maintain control over the salary bill in general.

Before leaving the subject of office personnel, some mention must be made of the terms of employment. These are more important than many people realise because, in effect, they constitute the basis of the contract of service which binds every employee to the firm.

The Contracts of Employment Act, 1963 places an obligation on the employer to provide a written statement for each employee, setting out clearly the terms governing his employment.

In view of the fact that the terms have legal force, a solicitor should always be consulted when they are framed in order to avoid omissions or ambiguities which might, at a later date, involve either the firm or the employee in considerable difficulty.

Our attention can now be diverted from the employee and turned once again to the office manager, who should by this time have at his disposal a well-situated office, efficiently laid out, adequately lit and ventilated. His staff should have been properly interviewed, have a knowledge of their terms of employment and should be fitted into the training scheme and salary scale. It is the office manager's job now to get the whole unit working.

Here again, thought and care given in advance will save many headaches at a later date and the office manager who appreciates this will examine, one by one, all the many jobs which his office will be required to carry out.

Some of these jobs will be the purest routine, some will require special aptitudes, while others will be such that they can only be reliably done by senior and experienced members of the staff.

The ideal, which can seldom be attained, is for every member of the staff to be permanently engaged on work slightly more difficult than he can comfortably manage. In this way, all are kept at the highest pitch of interest and enthusiasm. Some steps in this direction can be taken by the rotation of duties already mentioned; for the rest, the extent to which the ideal can be reached depends on the work, the staff and the office manager in individual cases.

The routine work of the office manager—dictating letters and memoranda, for example—falls within the technical side of his job while supervision of the staff is equally clearly within the managerial side. It forms, in fact, about the whole of office management.

To get the picture in perspective we must see the office manager at his desk, in close proximity to the general office where his clerks work. He knows what work his office-unit has to do, because he has been primed by the managing director on such items of policy as concern him. He knows, too, how his office-unit is to do its work because he has himself laid down methods based on his own training and experience. Finally he knows just where his own office-unit fits into the organisation, with whom it must co-operate, who is dependent on it and on whom it depends. With this information clear in his mind, he can devote himself to the task of office management.

Under this heading will fall the guiding and advising of employees, planning the work, issuing instructions and checking results, interpretation of policy, recording and maintaining discipline.

Taking these in order, we have already dealt with guiding and advising when discussing training over which, of course, the office manager will exercise supervision.

We have also discussed the planning of work and, by inference, the issuing of instructions and checking results. We have therefore left for consideration only the interpretation of policy, recording and the maintenance of discipline.

It is not possible, of course, to be very dogmatic on the interpretation of policy for the reason that no hard and fast rules can be laid down until the policy is known and the function of the individual office is determined. Nevertheless, interpreting policy can be likened to working out a route for a motor-car trip when the destination has been decided. The Board have decided the destination of the company and have given effect to this decision in company policy.

Thereafter the managing director has broken down broad policy into its constituent parts based on its relevance to each of the five major functions. These parts of policy are, for the office managers, destinations in themselves and it is for them to work out the best route by which they can reach the destination at the required time. This, for them, is interpretation of policy.

Recording comprises filing, charting and reporting to higher management on those matters for which the office is responsible. Again, there are as many methods as offices but, as has already been said, as much standard practice as possible should be laid down within each firm. This both simplifies the work within the office and facilitates the interchange of staff, when necessary, between one office and another.

Turning now to the maintenance of discipline, we come immediately up against the human factor in full force. As two chapters—XVII and XVIII—are devoted to this subject, not a great deal need be said here.

The office manager will bear in mind, though, that in maintaining discipline he will do more by example than he can ever hope to do by force. It is a golden rule that there can be no control without self-control and the manager with an ungovernable temper will never have a well-disciplined office, though, to outward appearances, this may not seem to be the case. Cowed employees are not disciplined employees nor, usually, are they loyal or, except in the manager's presence, hard-working.

All the tenets, all the books and all the study will never enable a manager to conduct a really first-class office unless he makes it a rule that, to his staff, he is always outwardly the same—calm, just, enthusiastic and himself the hardest worker of them all. This applies whether he has a headache, has been reprimanded by higher authority, feels tired or whether he is fit, healthy and full of energy. The staff should not be able to tell the difference.

He will, too, support his staff to the bitter end. Mistakes may be made from time to time and, occasionally, these may escape the attention of the office manager with the result that he is reprimanded. He will accept that reprimand as deserved by himself, as, indeed, it is since he is responsible for the results of the work in the office. He may go back and, if it be a case of carelessness, pass on the rebuke tenfold to the clerk responsible but he will not blame that clerk to anyone else;

this factor is quite one of the most important in ensuring loyalty.

Finally, something must be said of the need for periodical self-examination by the office manager. It is his job constantly to have in mind the aims of simplifying office procedure, developing the usefulness of the work, economising and increasing efficiency. He can best satisfy this requirement by taking an opportunity every six months or so to weigh up what he has achieved, what he is achieving and to compare this with what he wants to achieve. Someone will tell him sooner or later if he is not developing his office and it is far better that he should be the one to tell himself and do something about it first.

CHAPTER XII

The Management of the Factory—1

Factory management, in its widest sense, has been the subject for innumerable textbooks and its scope would be far beyond the capacity of two chapters here. We must remember, though, that in the foregoing pages, we have divorced management from technicality. We can, therefore, limit our consideration to those aspects of factory management which apply to all factories, irrespective of what the product is.

The factory, then, is the physical expression of the production function of management. It is the means whereby the policy of the Board is achieved in so far as this relates to production. This policy will lay down details of what is to be made, when it is to be made and at what price it is to be made. Given this, it is for the factory, operating under the control of a senior executive, to carry out its tasks. It will be as well to begin with an explanation as to how those tasks are defined and converted into actions.

The managing director will be responsible for interpreting company policy into terms of the various functions, and for issuing instructions to the functional executives. In the case of the factory, this individual will be the works manager.

In a small firm the works manager may be solely responsible for the further translation of those instructions into works activities; in the larger concerns he may have the advice and assistance of sub-departments such as a production control department, a planning office, an inspection department and a maintenance department. Whether, in fact, he is so assisted is a matter of degree; in any case the work entrusted to those departments must be done somehow. It is all a part of the production function.

There will, of course, be an automatic liaison in the first instance between the works manager and the Board in order to relate the type of factory, its plant and its size to the demands to be made on it. This will only apply fully when a new firm is starting production but it presents a number of factors which can most usefully be examined here.

It has been said that every business enterprise originally starts with an idea—an idea that a demand exists in such force that a profit can be made out of satisfying it.

Now that demand may be for a small number of luxury articles on which a handsome profit can be realised; alternatively it may be a demand for a large number of cheap articles to satisfy a wide public. Again, it may be an indeterminate demand for an entirely new product which has yet to be tested on the market. The nature of the demand to be met is, therefore, a governing factor in production.

If the demand be for a small quantity of a luxury product, craftsmanship may well be the most important consideration. The factory can be small, no great outlay on plant will be necessary.

If vast quantities of a cheap product are wanted, mechanisation must be carried as far as possible and a large factory built to house the machinery.

In the last instance—an untried product—an attempt must be made to reconcile these two extremes by taking a small factory with room for expansion if the product meets with growing appreciation.

Whatever the building used to house the factory, its layout will be a matter of deep consideration by the works manager. He will, if he be wise, try to achieve as smooth a flow of work as possible, remembering that any diversion of work from one route to another through the factory will involve waste of time and will increase the complexity of administration.

The ideal, only occasionally possible, would be a large factory on one floor with raw materials coming in at one end, passing from process to process to a finished goods store and delivery bay at the other end.

Unfortunately very few products lend themselves to such treatment. In many industries various processes are required for some products and not for others, factory buildings are not conveniently shaped, cost precludes one-floor construction and so on. Most works managers, therefore, have to do their best within the difficulties imposed on them.

Even so, a great deal can be done by careful study of a floor plan of the factory. On this can be marked in various colours the routes of the various products and any obvious hindrances to the smooth flow can be seen. To see them is a good deal of the way towards eradicating them.

If, in addition to the floor plan, pieces of coloured paper are cut to scale to represent the machines, tentative re-arrangements of plant can be tried out in the works manager's office in the certainty that any plan finally evolved will be workable.

No wise Board and, similarly, no wise works manager will be blind to the need for flexibility of plant. A demand to-day for one kind of product may well have changed or have become subject to acute competition in a few years' time. To have set up a one-purpose plant to meet such a demand would be to incur a complete re-equipment if this happened. Whenever possible, then, versatile machinery should form the basis of a progressive factory though, in appropriate cases, individual special-purpose machines can be a very useful adjunct to economical production.

There is one exception to this rule—mass production, which we shall discuss later. As will then be seen, special-purpose plant may well be essential. This, however, constitutes a special case.

Another factor of prime importance which can give rise to serious troubles if it be neglected is that of expansion.

Every firm starting in business probably envisages ultimately enlarging its activities either by producing more of one commodity or by branching out into the manufacture of allied commodities. Where this is the case, where management does envisage expansion, the time to think of it is when the plant is first set up.

Failure to do this means that, as soon as the firm begins to expand, pressure is put on the limited space available. More machines are crowded in, gangways are reduced, office space is contracted, welfare services are restricted until the limitation of bricks and mortar inevitably control the issue and further expansion becomes a physical impossibility.

The only ways of getting round this state of affairs are either by opening up additional plant somewhere else or by moving the whole existing plant to new and more commodious premises.

The former alternative may often seem the more simple since it involves no interruption of production and no expensive removal charges. It is usually true, though, that complete removal is, in the long run, the more economical step to take.

This is because of the difficulties of trying to conduct, from one centre, the activities of two or more producing units physically separated by, sometimes, many miles. Inevitable delays occur, instructions are misinterpreted and senior appointments have to be duplicated in order to maintain intact the chain of command. Thus a saving in initial expense may result eventually in a long-term drain on the resources of the company.

Opening up new factories and removing existing factories are, however, but expedients forced on managements who either have not foreseen future expansion or who, for a variety of reasons, have been unable to take future expansion sufficiently into account at the beginning of the project.

Wherever possible, future expansion should figure as an integral part of the considerations which must precede the setting up of any factory. Preference should be given, for example, to sites which permit of expansion, additional land may even be bought or leased against the time when it will be needed. Where buildings are being taken over the possibility of adding extra floors should not be overlooked.

I have mentioned development as one of the major functions of management. It is under the heading of development that expansion will find a place.

Unfortunately, the possibility of expansion is not the only factor to be considered when selecting a new site for a factory. There are innumerable others. So many are there, in fact, that it is probably true to say that no site is ideal on all counts. The most management can hope to do is to choose, of the sites available, the one which contains a maximum of desirable features and a minimum of undesirable ones.

A governing factor which will loom largely in any discussion on choice of site is the nature of the product and the raw materials from which it is made.

Where the raw materials are easily transported and the end-product fragile or perishable, there is little option but to choose a site near the ultimate market. Where the reverse applies and the product is easily transportable while the raw materials present transport difficulties, the practical solution will lie in choosing a site near the source of raw material supply.

Waste, or by-products, too, create an influence. Some processes throw off a semi-saleable by-product which is of insufficient value to justify special marketing. By siting the factory near others engaged in like processes, the combined by-products may well be sufficient to attract the attention of a dealer who will undertake his own collection and marketing.

Further arguments can be advanced in favour of siting a factory near others engaged in the same work. Labour supply, for instance, is probably simplified in that there is a greater likelihood of skilled and semi-skilled workers being available.

Liaison with suppliers of raw materials can, too, be more fully maintained where like factories are grouped. A supplier is much more likely to arrange for regular visits by his traveller when all the customers are in one place than he is when they are extended over the length and breadth of the country.

Lucky is the works manager who has a say in the choice of his factory's site, and who manages so far to reconcile the irreconcilables as to find one which really accords with his needs.

We must now assume that the site has been selected, the

plant installed, room left for expansion and a smooth flow of work arranged. The next thing to consider is the means whereby the whole concern is brought to life.

Just as finance is the life-blood which must be kept flowing at even pressure through the arteries of the business as a whole, so productive work is the life-blood necessary to the arteries of the factory. Without work to do the factory has no reason for existence ; with too much work for the capacity available the flow will become obstructed ; with too little work the full facilities—which are being paid for—will not yield adequate return. Work, then, in the form of production orders, must not only be provided but provided in a steady and regular flow. This, anyway, is the dream of every factory manager.

In order to achieve this even flow a great deal of pre-preparation must be applied to production orders before they reach the factory floor. Just to translate to a work docket anything and everything any customer asked for and to hand such work docket to the factory manager would be a fair way of creating chaos.

In discussing the pre-preparation which is necessary I am not, for the moment, considering where production orders originate. The point of origin may be the sales office, the Board or the factory or works manager himself. Consideration of this is, however, more appropriate to the succeeding chapter. For the moment, I am taking up the story of events from the point where authority to produce has been given.

The customer is not always the best judge of what he wants ; alternatively, he may be vague in his stated requirements. It is the job first of the designer to clarify these requirements and to ensure that the article to be produced will be such as to lend itself to the facilities available.

By this I don't mean that a man ordering ten thousand electric irons should be persuaded to accept instead fifty thousand electric kettles just because the factory is better equipped to produce the latter than the former.

I do mean, though, that an electric iron contains a number

of separate parts and by seeing to it that each of these parts is either standardised or capable of economic production the designer can very materially assist in ensuring smooth and simple production and in reducing cost.

Where the firm is engaged in pre-manufacture for later sale—that is, manufacturing for stock in advance of anticipated sales orders—the designer can play quite a distinct part, too, in making the article attractive to the consumer. Mainly, though, it is the designer's job to relate production requirements to production possibilities.

When his work is done, the product to be manufactured has been reduced to a set of drawings, a series of formulæ or a batch of works instructions probably quite unintelligible to the ultimate consumer but the very language of the factory.

From what has already been said about time and motion study and work measurement it should have been appreciated that, however complex a series of operations, each is capable of being isolated and measured. It follows that the length of time needed for the completion of each process can be assessed in advance. This is done by the planning office or production control department.

The position now is that the order, in the form of works instructions, is awaiting issue to the factory but, before issue, it must be fitted into the production plan. This is necessary for two reasons.

First, unless a plan is in being and is reasonably closely observed, no one—not even the works manager—will have any idea as to what is going on. Jobs will get side-tracked, mis-handled, delayed and forgotten ; unsuitable machinery will be used where the right machine is occupied doing unsuitable work ; in short, muddle will reign in the absence of any recognised plan of action.

Secondly, without a plan the planning office cannot tell whether work is on schedule or not and will thus be stultified in its attempt to keep other departments—sales, purchasing, costing and so on—posted as to progress and other matters of interest to them. With a plan, actual performance can be compared against planned performance and incipient departures of one from the other can be investigated before anything really harmful has happened.

So there must be a production plan.

There are various means of charting and recording factory capacity and its utilisation and no doubt each is right in its own sphere. Probably the bar chart is most widely used for machine loading purposes. Machine loading is the term used to describe the allotment of work to individual machines.

The bar chart, sometimes known as a Gantt chart, carries the types and numbers of all productive machines down the left-hand side, the space to the right being marked off in units of days or hours.

When a job timed to occupy, say, thirty hours, is allotted to a machine, a bar, carrying the job number and extending over thirty hourly units, is drawn or fixed mechanically to the chart opposite the number of the machine concerned. It is thus apparent at a glance that that machine has thirty hours' work ahead of it. Any additional work calling for the use of that machine must be scheduled to start after that thirty-hour period is expired.

Thus is built up a picture which, to the experienced eye, is even more illuminating than a tour round the factories. The man in charge can tell at once which machines are occupied, when they'll be available, the forward demand on the plant, and capacity available.

It is becoming increasingly the custom to promote the planning office into a more powerful and comprehensive unit by putting in its care the multiplicity of other activities which surround the transition of raw materials into the finished product. To mark this enhanced influence, the planning office is often re-styled the production control department.

By virtue of increased responsibility, the head of the production control department is a man able to assume quite a high place in the organisation structure of the business, ranking often immediately below the works manager and on a level with the production manager and chief engineer. It would be a brief description of his job to say that he makes himself responsible for all production documentation ; that is, all those activities attaching to work passing through the factory other than those of a mechanical or technical nature.

Assuming that there is a production control manager, he will receive in his office the instructions to put an order in hand. Before these instructions reach him, they will have been considered by the production manager who will have satisfied himself that the work can be done, how it can best be done, what alterations will be necessary to factory layout and, in fact, will have given his attention to all the technical considerations surrounding the production of the job. Where appropriate, his notes on the job will be attached to the instructions when they reach the production control manager. This latter individual, therefore, has before him all he needs to know in order to get the wheels turning, plan the work and progress it through the factory, however many processes may be involved.

Since nothing can be produced without raw materials these will be his first concern. Since, too, raw materials have often a substantial cash value, every care must surround their issue.

Sometimes, issue is made against unsupported requisitions —unit documents, signed by a foreman and passed to stores in return for the material specified. Seldom is this a system without its weaknesses. Requisitions get lost, they absorb considerable handling time and, worst of all, it is very difficult indeed to relate materials issued to materials required for the job. If materials are being drawn in penny numbers, no store-keeper can be expected to remember what each job requires and how much has been issued against each.

To improve this system, the production control manager supplies the store-keeper with a schedule showing, in the case of each job going forward, the total permitted issue of materials, listed item by item. With this in his possession, the store-keeper can issue the factory requirements on demand, obtaining a signature for each issue and marking the quantity on the schedule. When the permitted quantity has been reached, no more issues can be made without reference to the production control department. Waste, at a calculated rate, is, of course, allowed for in the schedule.

At the completion of each job—or batch, which we shall talk about in the next chapter—the material schedule is passed to the cost office where it affords a record of the materials issued for charging to the job.

Having dealt with materials, the production control manager has to fit each job into the factory schedule, using for this purpose his own knowledge of the plant available, modified where necessary by the noted requirements of the production manager.

From the chart already described, the unused capacity of each unit of plant can be seen at a glance ; into this unused capacity, the job in hand will be fitted, the chart being adjusted and the works instructions being endorsed with a note of the machines to be used and the order in which the job is to be taken.

After passing the job to the factory, the production control manager will then await his daily, or half-daily, reports on its progress. These may take the form of actual reports, but, more usually, information reaches the production control office by means of job records which have already served the purpose of keeping check on employees' activities and earnings. By routing these through the production control office a double purpose is achieved, since the progress of the work can be seen and the chart marked accordingly.

Only when a job is behind schedule will the production control manager take steps to chase it, or to enquire as to what is delaying it. With a well-working system, however, these occasions should be few.

It will be seen that the production control department is a watch tower from which can be organised and surveyed all factory activities. All questions as to the progress of jobs, the effect of revised instructions, cancellations, quantity increases and the like are referred to this office and there answered from information immediately available.

CHAPTER XIII

The Management of the Factory—2

In the last chapter reference was made to initiation of production and we are now to consider at what point in any manufacturing organisation production is initiated. Who, in other words, has the authority to say that production is to commence ?

Production may be initiated by the Board, the sales office or the works manager, depending upon the nature, or method, of production undertaken by the firm. This may be mass production, job production or batch production ; in each case initiation is authorised by a different individual. Each method, too, has its own qualifying factors.

Mass production is a term often wrongly applied to any industry where a conveyor belt is incorporated in the production line. True mass production is, in this country at least, rare.

This is so because mass production only becomes an economic method of manufacture when precise—and extensive—production needs can be seen a long time in advance. It is not only necessary to predict how much shall be produced, it is also necessary to establish in advance exactly what shall be produced in terms of design. Further, once mass production has been started, it becomes uneconomic to alter or modify any of the pre-planned details. The same identical article must be produced in a continuous flow until the scheduled quantity is complete.

There are very few industries which can predict, with any accuracy, the demand for their product over at least a year ahead. Of the few, there are still fewer which can safely lay down a standard design and adhere to it without variation. Finally, even where these conditions are satisfied, there must also be considered the need for a market so extensive as to be able to absorb the product in economic quantities.

Even so, there are some industries where all these possibilities exist—the motor-car industry is one—and in these cases, true mass production can be found.

One with even an elementary knowledge of factory management will clearly see that, if design and quantity of production can be rigidly fixed in advance and if large quantities of the product can be sold, the whole approach to production problems is fundamentally altered. The factory, as it were, can be constructed round the product.

Special machinery can be built, capable of performing one unchanging operation ; plant can be installed and sited to meet the requirement of one unchanging programme of production ; conveyor and handling equipment can be constructed and installed to eliminate as much manual lifting and moving as possible. In short, the whole production line can be set up with one product as the sole governing factor.

Building and siting special machines, though, is an expensive matter, as is the installation of built-in conveyors and hoists ; for this reason a very considerable amount of thought and planning must precede any mass production.

First must be decided the design of the product in the greatest detail and this must be related to the consumers' needs and to the mechanical demands of production.

This done, costs must be decided for varying levels of production. Here the works manager, cost accountant and others interested will get together and thrash out costs based on a range of output levels, the minimum being that below which mass production would be uneconomic and the maximum being the estimated capacity of the factory.

In our discussion on costing, it will be recalled, it was explained that cost per unit tended to fall as output increased, since static overhead expenses are borne by a greater number of units. This being so, the range of cost figures for the mass produced article will begin with a minimum number of high-cost articles and progress by stages to a maximum number of low-cost articles.

At this point the sales manager and his market research advisers come into the picture. It is for them to say how many articles can be sold, basing their contention on the prices.

Knowing the extent of competition, consumer demand as measured in various areas and probable unabsorbed consumer capacity, a quantity will be selected which will form the basis of the production schedule.

It is the managing director who has to co-ordinate all these pieces of advice and technical opinion and to reconcile one with another until he is satisfied that a production programme can be laid down. He reports accordingly to the Board who, after examining the whole project in detail, authorise production to start.

On receipt of this sanction, the machinery can be installed, the production line laid down, materials can be bought and in due course production commences and the pipe-lines of distribution begin to pour out the finished article to the market. Once started, however, any variation in a design or quantity must be vigorously avoided as the economics of the whole project depend on an uninterrupted flow throughout the whole programme.

In the case of mass production, then, the Board initiate production ; it is the Board which gives the instructions to commence work.

Job production is a very different matter. Job production is the method used by the substantial majority of small factories throughout the country, each working in accordance with customers' orders. The printer, the bespoke tailor, the garage, the small engineering shop, all these are working on job production.

It is a feature of job production that nothing can be produced until a customer places an order and, within varying limits, there is no means of knowing in advance what the customer will order.

For this reason the job production factory must have as

versatile a plant as possible, able to cope with a wide variety of potential customers' orders. Special-purpose plant is out of the question, as also are fixed conveyor belts and internal transport gear, except such as will meet an infinity of different requirements.

The lay-out of the plant must be so arranged that almost any plan of work-flow can be accommodated and, of course, the office routine must be similarly adaptable.

Since production cannot start until an order is received, it is the sales office who initiate production. This initiation, of course, takes place on the delegated authority of the Board but, nevertheless, from the works manager's point of view, it is to the sales office that he looks for instructions.

Sometimes, where no extensive technicalities are involved, the works orders can be issued direct from the sales office. In other industries, the sales office issue an order to the production control department. Here the customer's requirements are translated into technical terms before issue to the works in the form of a works order or work docket. The authority to initiate production is, however, still vested in the sales office.

Batch production, in its more advanced forms, is often miscalled mass production by those unversed in factory lore. In fact, batch production is more closely related to job production.

Batch production is the method of production used by factories which rely for their livelihood on customers' orders in advance—as in the case of job production factories—but which are accustomed to receive those orders in the form of contracts. Additionally, it is applicable to factories in which individual jobs can be grouped in like kinds for manufacturing purposes.

By way of examples, I can mention the tin-box manufacturers who receive orders for, perhaps, so many million tins of a certain size and specification to be delivered to the customer in a series of deliveries spread over a year ; or the clothing factory where individual orders can be grouped for some operation, such as making up. In both these cases, and thousands like them, batch production is the method used.

In a batch production factory, a certain amount of special-purpose plant can be used and there can be more rigidity in the factory lay-out than is appropriate to the job production factory. Even so, much of the flexibility of the job production method must be retained for the reason that it is still the customer who states his requirements; it is not for the Board to relate plant to output as in the case of mass production factories.

Under batch production conditions, it is again the sales office which receive the original order from the customer, but it is not the sales office which initiate production. This is the works manager's responsibility.

The customer's requirements are transmitted by the sales office to the production control department or direct to the works manager. Having been assured that the delivery dates and quantities will be adhered to, the sales office are no longer concerned with the order.

The works manager, however, must now decide how he is going to work the job. If, for instance, a customer has ordered six million tins to be delivered at the rate of half a million a month, it will clearly be uneconomic to make the six million all in one batch and store them against the successive delivery dates. Rent of storage space alone would prohibit this.

On the other hand, setting up the machines and adjusting the lay-out to make the tins may be a reasonably extended process. To do this every month to make half a million tins might well so increase the cost per tin that production would itself become uneconomic. The works manager, therefore, must reconcile, with the aid of the cost accountant, the various conflicting factors. These will include the make-ready time, the rent of storage space and the demands of other customers to which he is committed. After working all this out, he will have decided on the most economical batch-size. He may decide, for example, to make a million tins every second month, storing half a million at a time or, if storage rental is low and make-ready costs high, he may decide to work batches of two million tins every four months.

Having decided his batch-sizes, the work is fed into the factory at the instigation of the works manager who, in effect, initiates production.

I have described mass, job and batch production as separate methods because it is easier to explain them in this way. It must be understood, though, that the three methods are commonly found in operation at the same time in the same factory.

A motor-car manufacturer, for example, may employ mass production methods for his main assembly, batch production methods for the manufacture of components and job production methods for special orders, maintenance work and the like.

Similarly, the small job production factory may have a few contracts which justify batch production procedure and this method may then be introduced alongside the job production routine more usual to the undertaking.

Whatever the method of production and whatever the product, the control of the factory must be in accordance with standard management practice, the rules of responsibility and authority being scrupulously obeyed at all levels of management.

Since the factory proper is a part of the production function, it will come under the control of the specialist executive responsible for that function. He will probably be known as the works manager, factory manager, general works manager or production manager. His title matters little.

What does matter is that he shall be possessed of technical skill in the processes employed in the factory and, additionally, that he shall be adept at management. His job, as we have seen, will be to receive broad instructions as to policy from the managing director and instruction as to what is required from either the Board or the sales office. These instructions he will convert into finished goods at a cost such that the sales policy can be achieved. In addition, as a specialist in production, he will advise his colleagues and the

Board, through the managing director, on all technical matters relevant to his function and, in the case of batch production, will initiate this himself.

Although he must be a technical man, he is situated near the top of the management hierarchy and, by previous definition, his actual job will be a predominantly managing one, not a technical one. In short, the majority of his time will be spent in directing human activities, a minority only being devoted to technical pursuits.

Even in a small factory, it is seldom possible for the works manager to give individual attention to each subordinate employee and where such employees number more than half a dozen or so, they become numerically beyond the span of control doctrine which teaches that no man can adequately exercise direct supervision over and responsibility for the work of more than five or six subordinates. It is necessary, then, to group the subordinates under the care of individuals who, themselves, are in direct touch with the works manager.

The number of these intermediaries will vary according to the total numbers employed and the number of departments or sections into which the productive unit is divided.

Taking as an illustration a very large organisation, there might be five factory supervisors reporting direct to the works manager and each in charge of a factory.

Each supervisor would then exercise control over his leading foremen, each, again, with five or fewer foremen responsible to him. Each foreman at the lower level might then be responsible for directing the activities of five chargehands, each in charge of one or more sections, each section being in the care of a section hand. Only at this lowest level is it occasionally permissible to exceed the span of control but, even then, a section hand should not have more than a dozen workers responsible to him.

At this level, the job of the section hand is almost wholly technical and management, or the direction of the activities of his workers, plays a very small part in his job. Primarily, the section hand works on a machine or at the bench. Beyond seeing that his section knows, individually, what to do, that each is doing his job and beyond referring to his superior any queries that may arise, the section hand has little to distinguish his job from that of the worker. For this reason—that management plays a very small part in the section hand's work—the span of control may be exceeded without detriment to the chain of command.

This is the sort of organisation that one might expect to find in a large industrial plant. In a small firm the works manager may find two or three overseers or foremen quite sufficient for his purpose, but if he finds he needs more than five he should give earnest consideration to the advisability of breaking down the organisation into smaller units and creating a lower level of command, subordinate to the foremen. In this way he can preserve the span of control and, with it, his own ability to control effectively.

The span of control, though, is only the outward and apparent means by which control is exercised; more important is the managerial ability of the works manager, foremen and chargehands—all those, in fact, who practise management, whatever the level.

It is no good at all setting up a carefully balanced organisation, observing the span of control at all levels, if the works manager is repeatedly going to short-circuit his own foremen and pass instructions directly to the operatives or if the foremen themselves have little clear idea of the extent of their responsibility and authority.

As in all management, the works manager and all below him must have a crystal-clear idea of whence their instructions will come, to what extent they, personally, are responsible for carrying them out, the authority they possess to make this possible and the person to whom they report when necessary. If all are clear on these fundamental matters, little can upset the even running of the production unit.

Perhaps one of the most common failings to be found among works managers is the inability to shed themselves of responsibility and authority by passing down responsibility and by delegating the concomitant authority.

It is easy to see that a man who has started at the bottom and worked his way up to a works manager's office will tend to be obsessed with the idea that he alone can do a job properly ; here lies the danger.

At every stage on the upward climb the manager must examine his job closely and impartially, asking himself just how much of his work at that stage could be done by a subordinate. If he fails to do this, he will either fail to achieve further promotion or, perhaps worse, he will arrive at the top so cluttered up with a host of detail that he will be scarcely able to do any management at all.

The wise man, who has taken pains to relieve himself of detailed work by passing it down to his subordinates at all stages, will reach the full stature of management, able to devote his time to clear thinking, development and, of course, managing.

Before passing on, I should perhaps make it clear that, by passing down responsibility and authority in respect of detail, the works manager does not absolve himself from blame if anything goes wrong. He is, and must always be, solely responsible to the managing director for the activities of his function. He cannot meet trouble by blaming a foreman to whom he has entrusted some part of his responsibility. He must answer personally for any mistake, but he can say what he likes to the foreman afterwards.

In addition to running the factory the works manager will have, of course, constant liaison with his own advisory departments, production control, drawing office, planning, stores, maintenance and like departments as well as with the other functional departments of the business.

He will usually work closely with the sales office as the interpreter of what the customer really wants ; with the personnel department in order that it may recruit the sort of personnel he needs ; with the development department so as to keep abreast, himself, of the latest developments in the technical field and so as to keep the development department apprised as to the most fruitful lines along which research might be conducted ; and with the accounts department in order to isolate, and at once examine, any departure from economical production.

For this last-named purpose, the information will probably emerge from the cost office where, as one of the integral parts of the work, actual costs will be carefully scrutinised against estimates. Any discrepancy will be brought to the attention of the works manager.

Similarly, it will be among the duties of the cost office to relate actual production, week by week, to potential production. Information such as this will, in fact, be thrown up by the normal working of the costing system. From it, the cost office will provide for the works manager a series of periodical efficiency ratios for each distinguishable section of the factory.

On receiving intimation that costs are too high or efficiency is too low, it will be for the works manager to consult with his next subordinate and pass the information down to the man at whose door delegated responsibility for the trouble lies. On his report the works manager will decide what, if any, action to take.

Before leaving the factory, I should say something about inspection, a sub-function around which a great deal of trouble has, from time to time, circulated.

Clearly, however it be organised, there must be some means of inspecting the work before it is finally passed out of the factory to the consumer.

In a host of small firms the foreman or overseer is, in effect, the inspector. He is responsible for seeing that finished work is up to standard. Any complaint from the customer is passed to him and it is for him to justify himself if he can. Incidentally, this is another case where the works manager takes what blame there is ; the foreman is responsible to the works manager, not to the customer.

In large firms, inspection assumes such proportions that a special inspection department is justified—and it is in connection with this that difficulties arise. Who is to take charge of it at top level ?

In order to understand the principle involved, it is

necessary first to look carefully into what an inspection department does. It is usually in the charge of a chief inspector who has under him one or more inspectors.

It is the duty of all these to examine the work passing through the factory at various stages. This examination may be an arbitrary one for quality of workmanship or it may be a positive one, carried out by means of gauges and measuring instruments. In either case it happens that, from time to time, part-finished and completed products are rejected as sub-standard.

Naturally, someone is to blame for the bad workmanship. It may be the man on the machine, it may be the setter, it may be the raw material supplier or it may be that wrong instructions have been issued. In any case, there is a tendency for one person to pass the blame to another.

Now the chief inspector's job is to certify that the work must be rejected, and to indicate where, in his opinion, the fault lies. For this reason it is of extreme importance that the inspection department should derive its authority from, for preference, the highest level—that is, the managing director himself.

If, as is often the case, the inspection department is considered a sub-function of production, deriving its authority from the works manager, trouble will instantly arise when the blame for the production of faulty goods is traceable to the works manager himself. The chief inspector is faced with an unenviable decision to make. His professional integrity and his duty to his company indicate that he shall lay the blame where it belongs; his loyalty to his own superior indicates otherwise.

To avoid these invidious situations, it is better to give the chief inspector a position in the organisation parallel with, and equal to, that of the works manager, with authority derived from the managing director.

An alternative sometimes used is to appoint a chief engineer or technician as a senior executive and to give him responsibility for inspection, maintenance, repairs and such other duties as lie only partly within the true production activities of the works manager.

No doubt there will be other means of fitting the inspection department into the organisation. All will be equally satisfactory as long as they observe the doctrine that no man can serve two masters.

CHAPTER XIV

Disposing of the Product

There are those who will argue that the distribution function, or that which concerns the disposal of the product, is the most important. All the resources of the producing unit, they would say, all the financial, psychological, mechanical and managerial means employed in giving birth to the product have, in effect, but one aim—to sell it.

This, I suggest with respect, is a misconception which, if widely held, can cause grave disaffection. No one function must be regarded as any more important than any other. Each function has a part to play in the team effort which is characteristic of every successful firm. Each is interdependent on the others, just as all the parts of a watch are equally necessary, irrespective of the size or precise purpose of each.

The distribution function embraces a number of separate activities, the collective purpose of which is to transfer the finished product into the hands of the consumer.

As in the case of the other functions, many of these activities are technical, others are the activities of human beings. In so far as the performance of the function involves directing the latter, to that extent it is a function of management.

The technical activities will include, possibly, tendering, technical representation, the preparation of technical advertising and sales promotion copy; the managerial activities will include the direction of technical and non-technical human beings in such a way as to give effect to the sales policy of the business.

Before anything at all can be sold, a market for it must be found. This is true of all products and of all methods of production, from the small man relying on a continuous run of orders to keep his job-production plant going to the large mass production manufacturer who must assess his market in the most detailed terms before even setting up his plant.

Now finding a market means a great deal more than deciding what group of people is most likely to consume any given product. It is necessary, broadly, to find out what can be sold, who will buy it, at what price they will buy it, in what quantities, how often and what competition already exists. Market research is the technique devised to answer all these questions.

Market research is not a technique to be applied without training, nor is it one to be applied loosely to each and every question agitating the manufacturer's mind.

Nevertheless, market research can be of the utmost value, properly applied, if it be limited to a research into an existing state of affairs; it becomes less reliable when used as a basis for the prediction of a future state of affairs. For example, a market research aimed at finding out how many people use a certain cleansing powder might well meet with outstanding success. A market research aimed at finding out how many people would use a certain cleansing powder if the price were reduced would be an unreliable basis for prediction. A consumer knows what he is using; he does not know what factors would guide him in his future purchases.

Market research is, then, the job of a specialist who derives his authority from the sales director and advises him and, through him, the managing director on procedure to be adopted, on how the research is to be carried out. Once completed, the specialist correlates the results and provides the statistical evidence on which future sales policy is based. Since the technique of market research is a technical and not a managerial occupation, only a brief outline of it will suffice here. It is not necessary for the sales manager himself to be a trained market research investigator but—and this is the management part of the job—he must know how to direct the activities of such an investigator. He must be in the position of a man who knows how to use a tool without having to know how that tool actually works. It will, therefore, be sufficient to show how market research is used.

In order to assess accurately a nation-wide market, it is not necessary to approach every potential consumer and to elicit from each a series of facts relative to the product. Were such an extensive operation necessary, market research would be a useless theory with no practical application.

The population of the country is divisible into a number of categories, to each of which a numerical value can be attributed. There are, for instance, so many earning over £3,000 per annum, so many earning between £1,000 and £3,000 per annum, and yet another proportion earning less than £1,000 per annum.

The population can also be divided up into those who live in houses and those who live in flats; into car-owners and those not possessing cars; into those owning their own houses and those renting accommodation; into urban, suburban and rural groups. In fact, evidence is in existence from which can be deduced almost any classification of the public. The market research man must decide which particular classifications are best suited to his needs.

If he is investigating the market for a motor-car accessory, he will obviously be concerned with the distribution, number and approximate incomes of car-owners. If, on the other hand, he is interested in electrical equipment, his concern will be with householders receiving main electricity supplies. These are but two examples to indicate the need for careful selection of the potential market.

Having established the numerical strength of the various groups comprising the market to be surveyed, the market analyst uses further references in order to find a suitable sample area.

A sample area is a district or locality in which the distribution of population relates as closely as possible to the national distribution in terms of income, professional status, housing, car-owning, television-viewing and the like. It is thus a miniature sample of the national market and conclusions drawn from the sample can be applied on a national scale.

The area decided, the next stage is to prepare a questionary to be used by the investigators. This consists of a number of questions which the investigator will put to selected persons in the chosen area. The object of these questions will be to ascertain what competitive product, if any, is being used, why it is being used, why it is bought and to elicit any opinion as to possible improvement which the consumer can suggest. Where the research is related to an existing product, much care will be devoted to finding out where, and why, it is not being used.

In preparing the questionary, the questions should be so framed that the answers can be coded for use on sorting and tabulating equipment. This is not completely possible, especially when opinions are being sought, but a great many questions can be so drafted that the answer will be an unqualified positive or negative.

The investigators now set out, equipped with a supply of questionaries and instructed as to the number and type of houses they are to call at. Some, too, will be equipped with a modified form of questionary and will be instructed to call on retailers and suppliers in the selected sample area.

In due course the completed questionaries—sometimes several thousand of them—are received back from the investigators and the job of correlating their information begins.

If the questionary has been expertly compiled, the completed papers will provide a very exhaustive source of information from which valuable conclusions can be drawn as to the extent and nature of the potential market in the sample area. By transferring the answers on to punched cards and sorting and tabulating them in a variety of different ways, a wealth of vital statistical guidance can be produced. From this the sales manager can assess what competition he must face, what the potentialities of the market are, what his selling price must be and, among many other things, the most profitable classification of consumer.

Since the sample area has been carefully chosen as representative of the national composition of the potential market, a sales policy based on the sample area findings should be applicable to the country as a whole. It is true that the direct application of sample area findings to national problems might prove of doubtful validity but it must not be forgotten that the questionaries are assessed and evaluated by highly skilled people who are well able to make such adjustments as may be necessary to relate the sample to the whole.

I have already made at some length the point that all good management depends in a large measure on an ability to predict future events. This applies with equal force to sales management and the sales manager, therefore, must use his market research data as a means of ascertaining the future needs of his potential consumers.

Analysis of this data will provide him with a clear indication of these needs, and from the same source he will have an idea of the price at which he must sell in order to cope with competition.

He will also know the income brackets, social standing, location and interest of those most likely to be the most lucrative section of the consuming public.

Classification of all these factors will indicate how his marketing is to be organised. He will be guided in the matter of packaging—whether it is to be expensive and attractive or cheap and merely serviceable.

He will also be guided in preparing his advertising and sales promotion campaigns, about which I shall have more to say later. For the moment it will be sufficient to draw attention to the obvious fact that advertising copy written for a low-income readership in the national press differs materially from copy written to attract sales from high-income readers of the more exclusive and expensive periodicals.

Before dealing with advertising, however, reference must be made to the selling organisation which will be responsible for making the sales, recording them and, in a general sense, distributing the product.

The size of the selling organisation and its nature must depend on the area to be covered and the type of product being sold.

A small firm working within a limited sales area in close proximity to the source of manufacture will be able to manage with, perhaps, a sales manager, two or three travellers and a few clerks. In this case, the sales manager himself will undertake the market research which will be greatly simplified when applied to so small a potential market.

Should such a small firm feel the need for a more experienced approach to market research, or advertising for that matter, the services of specialist firms are available.

The large firm with a nation-wide distribution area will need to have a much more fully-equipped selling organisation possessing, quite probably, a market research expert, an advertising manager, an export manager, two or three area managers, a contract manager and other specialist executives all under the authority of a sales manager. In this case, such a sales manager need know little of the individual techniques applied by his subordinates. He will, in fact, be required to practise nearly pure management in directing the activities of so many specialists.

Whether large or small, the selling organisation takes the same form with the sales manager at the head, advised, where appropriate, by such experts as he needs. Below him are his office personnel and his field force—or the travellers who make contact with the customers. Additionally, there may be a despatch organisation, though this is often more conveniently attached to the production function.

The organisation and operation of the clerical side of the sales office conforms to the general considerations that have already been discussed in Chapters X and XI. It remains to deal with the organisation of the field force.

The number of travellers will depend, of course, on the area to be covered and, wherever possible, this area should be divided into territories, clearly defined. To each territory an allotment of one or more travellers is made. This method of decentralisation has many merits; it simplifies working, provides an incentive for the travellers themselves and, even more important, affords means of comparison of the utmost value to the sales manager.

In the small firm working in a very limited area, separate territories may not be possible, the whole sales area being regarded as one territory.

In the large firm, the travellers will spend most of their time in their territories, reporting back only weekly or monthly in person to head office; at other times, probably daily, they will make written reports.

The form of these written reports is, all too often, a standard one calling for details of calls made and orders and enquiries obtained. Such reports are, as a result, little more than supporting documents to the expense account. It should be more widely realised that a comprehensive report can play a signal part in the implementation of sales policy.

A traveller's job is, in effect, a double one. He is charged with spreading information about the firm and its products throughout his territory; he is also charged—or should be charged—with providing a constant flow of inward information to his firm about his territory. It is this latter aspect of his job which is so often neglected.

The best market research can only indicate a state of affairs existing at the time the research is made. It is static and, unless repeated regularly, must become out of date and thus lose its value.

In the travellers, however, covering the whole sales area, large or small, there exists a ready-made means of keeping that market research up to date. To effect this, it is necessary to amplify the weekly report and to encourage, by means financial and otherwise, the inward flow of information.

A traveller doesn't spend his whole time interviewing potential customers. He travels about, he usually has some social side to his life, he uses restaurants, clubs and hotels where people meet. He is, in short, admirably fitted to glean information of the greatest value to head office and the sales manager. He must be taught to glean it.

The first step in this direction will be to provide ample spaces in the report forms for items of news; secondly, the traveller must be told to use them and encouraged to do so.

Some sales managers call all their salesmen in to head

office at regular intervals and use the occasion to address them, explaining as fully as possible the need, at head office, for advance information as to any changes in a territory likely to lead to an increase or decrease of business. Such an occasion can also be used for drawing attention to any particularly helpful reports recently received together with the action taken and results achieved. Properly encouraged, by exhortation and, where possible, financial reward, the salesmen can be educated to think on head office lines and become, in effect, an extension of head office in each territory.

Much harm is done, albeit thoughtlessly, by writing from head office direct to customers without advising the appropriate salesman. Attention to this must be given in any selling organisation.

Nothing is more unsettling to a salesman than to be confronted by a customer with some statement from head office which has not passed through the salesman's hands at all. He is at once put in a weak position and he is scarcely to be blamed if he harbours some hard thoughts about the people who take action over his head.

To avoid this, all communication between head office and customer should be conducted through the salesman. Where this is impossible—as for instance when, for prestige reasons, it is necessary for the sales manager to write a personal letter to a customer—a copy of the letter and copies of all subsequent correspondence should be sent without delay to the salesman on the spot. He is thus constantly kept aware of all that is happening.

The field force, or the salesmen on their rounds, do not constitute the whole of the selling organisation. They must be backed up by a first-class service operated from head office.

From this source they should be kept regularly supplied with all the latest information regarding product, prices, competition, delivery dates and with details of their own activities in terms of turnover, number of orders, number of enquiries and the like. By comparing these with figures of previous years, a sense of competition is engendered which may, with some salesmen, prove a powerful stimulus to greater effort.

Naturally, the filing systems and methods of documentation at head office will be such that any query from a salesman can be answered with the least possible delay. Provision should also be made, too, for a regular survey of estimates given and orders received. Any estimate not resulting in an order may well repay careful investigation. Carried out at frequent intervals, the classified results of such surveys can often draw attention to shortcomings in the pricing and selling methods which, otherwise, might go unremarked for many years.

The sales manager and his organisation will have a large part to play in the price-fixing policy of the firm. Earlier, I tried to explain that prices fix costs; it therefore behoves the sales manager to pay particular attention to the prices charged for the firm's products.

He will be materially helped in his decisions and in the advice he gives his management by the salemen's reports already discussed. From these he will know what price-competition his firm is up against and should be able to set a value on that imponderable quality known as "service to the consumer". His aim, of course, is to set a price on the products such that the greatest possible proportion of potential output can be sold. To set such a price is not easy under any circumstances; it is nearly impossible unless the sales manager is in direct and intimate touch with his field force.

Before passing on from discussion of the selling organisation, a word should be said about the salesmen's remuneration.

There are still cases, though they are diminishing, where the employer expects the salesman to prove his worth at his own expense. The salesman is paid little or no salary but moderately generous commission on the sales he books. True, a really good salesman can earn a substantial salary by these means but it is not a practice to be commended. It can never engender loyalty or respect for the employer; it must result in a heavy turnover of sales staff and, since it offers no sense of security, it cannot breed what every sales manager wants, a happy and contented team.

It follows that any salesman employed primarily on a commission basis is at the mercy of every slump, of ill health, accident and other causes outside his control, any of which may reduce his income below the poverty line. He cannot, therefore, be a good advertisement for his employer whose reputation among his customers is largely based on the presence and loyalty of the salesman.

Many experienced sales managers recognise this and themselves accept responsibility for engaging the salesman by paying him, as salary, a living wage plus commission at a rate such as to form an incentive but no more. The firm having appointed the salesman backs its own judgement, as it were, and does not put all the onus of proving himself on the salesman.

I pass on now to some notes on the subject of advertising and sales promotion—the physical means whereby the personal approach of the salesman is supported and enhanced. Let me say at once that advertising and salesmanship are no substitute for each other; they are complementary.

An advertising campaign, ill-supported by salesmanship at the point of sale, is even more likely to prove a costly failure than is good salesmanship lacking advertising support. Further be it noted, neither advertising nor salesmanship, however good, however well dovetailed, will consistently sell a bad article.

The various advertising media are already well known; the national and local press, television, periodicals, hoardings, films, radio and, finally, direct mail.

Each method of advertising has its own sphere in which it can achieve the most telling effect; several methods are commonly used jointly as in the case of a press campaign backed by television and posters and linked by a coupon system to direct mail.

Before deciding which method he is to use, the sales manager will need to consider carefully the relationship between the cost of the campaign and the results he expects to achieve. If he is selling a product of national consumption, a big press and television campaign may be justified, however expensive.

If, on the other hand, he is a small man selling locally and unable or unwilling to expand his output, a direct mail campaign backed by a few posters, some small insertions in the local press and some screen time at his local cinema may well achieve all he wants. In finding his direct mail address list, he will, of course, apply a market research analysis to the possible addresses, thus eliminating, as far as possible, the wastage of his literature on persons never likely to need his products.

Problems connected with dispatch services are unlikely to trouble the sales manager of any but the largest concerns, in which, of course, a dispatch or transport manager will be one of the advisory executives subordinate to the sales manager.

In the smaller firms, the physical transport of the goods from factory to consumer is usually organised under the production function, the sales manager's part being completed when he has received the order and passed it to the factory. It matters little, though, who organises the dispatch service as long as it is quite clear to all where the responsibility lies.

Whoever is in charge will have many factors to consider and he will be guided in his decision by the nature of the product and of the service rendered by the company. He will have to weigh up the relative advantages and disadvantages of possessing a fleet of lorries, hiring lorries as required, contracting for lorries, using existing road transport services, using rail transport or, on occasion, air, sea or canal transport, operating a few small vans or a complex organisation incorporating all of these methods.

The probability is that each contract or order will ideally call for a different method. The bulky load to the other end of the country, the compact load for the next town, the samples wanted overseas urgently, the fragile load for piece-meal delivery—all these present their own problems and, clearly, deep thought must be devoted to finding the best compromise between all the alternatives offered.

CHAPTER XV

Developing the Undertaking

Of all the five major functions of management, development is the one most neglected. Selling, production, finance all clearly need constant attention ; they are, as it were, the visible functions which are apparent to everyone, manager or not.

Personnel relations, not quite such a visible function, nevertheless very soon becomes one if it be neglected. Realisation is now rapidly spreading that the time to stop industrial unrest is before it starts ; for that reason personnel managers are being appointed to take care of this function.

But the neglect of development seldom has any immediate repercussions. The results of such neglect are insidious, slow and often invisible to the man on the spot. Only when neglect has been allowed to go on for years does the day of reckoning dawn too late.

Yet it should be obvious that anything which does not receive care or attention must, in the very nature of things, deteriorate. This is as true of the Albert Memorial as it is of a pair of trousers ; as true of Cleopatra's Needle as of a business. Unless it be someone's specific job to see that a business is kept abreast of its competitors, that business will surely deteriorate and decline.

Note that it is not merely necessary to avoid slipping backward ; it is necessary positively to develop the business if it is to maintain its place in face of competition. Competitors will be developing, new ideas will be making their appearance and new methods will be becoming practical. The firm that just stands still, therefore, is, in relation to its industry, being left behind.

For this reason, increasing attention is being given to

development as a major function in the care of an executive responsible for seeing that his firm is at all times abreast of events and at all times ready to advance along pre-arranged lines of policy.

Such an executive has a job rather different from those of his colleagues who are concerned mainly with the day-to-day operation of the business. The development—or research—manager is mainly concerned with the operation of the business five, ten, even fifteen years ahead. What is happening to-day doesn't interest him ; he should have considered it years ago.

His job, too, is a manifold one though all its activities are clearly definable as part of development, thus preserving the nature of the function. He may be concerned with mechanical development, research into new processes, research into new markets, research into new manufactures by new methods, research into the future organisation of the company, research into possible expansion and research into all those problems which, if solved before they occur, can vastly simplify the work of the managing director and the other executives.

The development manager, therefore, is not quite so limited in his scope as are his colleagues. His activities touch on production, selling, finance and personnel relations but, and this is the important thing, only in so far as those functions must develop in step with each other. He will not try and run the personnel department, for instance, but he will be immensely interested in the plans laid for training and grooming those destined to replace the senior executives when the time comes for them to retire.

By the same token he will not presume to advise the works manager or production manager on matters concerned with new plant ; he will, though, see to it that all interested are kept well aware of what is available, of what new thought is taking place and of general development matters which it is his province, as development manager, to watch and assess.

As in the case of the other functions, it is only the substantial concerns who can justify the services of a full-time development manager, responsible, often, for the activities of a team of technicians, chemists, physicists and the like. In the smaller unit, the responsibility for watching development must devolve as a part-time duty on one of the directors, the works manager, the maintenance engineer or some other official constitutionally and technically equipped to bring the right quality of thought to bear on it. The important thing is to ensure that development is the responsibility of one individual and that it is not left loosely in the hands of several. Whether he be part-time or full-time, there must exist a development manager in practice, if not in name.

Success in his job will depend on his ability to cast his mind forward and to see his firm as it will be in five, ten or fifteen years' time. Everyone employed will cheerfully admit that changes in mechanical, technical and organisational directions will take place in the future ; it is the development manager's job to see to it that these changes take place in ordered sequence, that they are the right changes, that they accord with policy and that they take place at the will of the Board. Changes, however good, forced on a company by outside competitive influences must lose most of their advantages.

The development manager, then, must be constantly attuned to research—technical research, management research and market research, bearing in mind the whole time that his purpose is a long-term one. He is less interested in the potential number of customers in Yorkshire to-day than he is in the possibility of a new market arising in Canada five years hence. He is less interested in what the Yorkshire consumer wants now than in the modifications necessary in the product to make it popular in an eventual Canadian market. This example will, I think, serve to differentiate between research as understood by a development manager and research as practised by his colleagues in the course of their duties.

In a large organisation considerable sums can be profitably and economically spent on research. Laboratories and test-benches can be set up, pilot plants constructed, skilled brains enlisted in the knowledge that the rewards of successful research will be substantial and in the knowledge that the costs of such research can be absorbed comfortably into the economic price of the product.

In a small firm, however, with a modest annual turnover, lavish expenditure on development research can seldom be justified—but this does not mean that it must be ignored.

Where an industry is close knit, immense advantages can accrue from the setting up of a joint research station to study the technical problems of the whole industry and to make its findings correspondingly available. In this way, for a reasonable annual subscription, the smallest firm in the industry can have at call the research services of the most brilliant specialist brains.

In other cases, the consultant services of research organisations can be secured at moderate cost for the purpose of investigating specific problems. This, however, is only to consider part of the development manager's function.

In addition to availing himself of all the technical research facilities open to him, he will study the trade press of the world, read extensively all the technical publications he can get and, all the time, digest what he is reading in terms of the future.

Thus equipped, he should be able to judge the potentialities of any new process or machine long before his competitors have seriously considered any change. Knowledge of the possibilities and limitations of any new departure makes relatively simple the decision of the Board when the time comes to consider new equipment or expansion.

Parallel with research into technical improvements the development manager must give his mind to the markets his firm serves and hopes to serve. I have already referred, in passing, to this and have drawn attention to the ever-present need for exploring new outlets for the product.

This is necessary both to replace existing markets which may be lost and to cope with increased production from an expanding organisation. Not only will new potential markets be needed, but the requirements of these markets will have to be studied.

Here the development manager will form the apex of a triangle of which the two other angles are the works manager and the sales manager. Together, these three will co-operate to work out problems of product design for the future markets to be opened up.

Broadly, the development manager will explore the potentialities of various new markets, the sales manager will bring to bear his specialist knowledge of what those markets are likely to need and the works manager, with his technical ability, will relate these needs in terms of quantity and design to the production facilities available. Plans are thus jointly laid for future sales development.

Additionally to seeking new outlets for existing products and finding new products for existing outlets, many a development manager has earned the gratitude of his company by finding a market for hitherto wasted by-products.

This, of course, involves technical research of a high order but is well worth while in the case of any industry in which by-products are thrown out in quantity and are costly to disperse.

In relation to the conservation, or accounting, function, the activities of the development manager will not be so pronounced. There will, however, be a close liaison when the development manager is turning his mind to possibilities of future expansion.

By virtue of the fact that the development manager's thought processes are projected into the future, his activities are mainly in the realms of planning. Once he has laid his plans, checked them, convinced the Board of their advantages and practicability and had them approved, he, in his functional capacity, loses practical interest in them. The plans, by that time, have become matters of technical application and, as such, pass out of the hands of the development manager to those of the other functional executives whose duty it now is, in their separate capacities, to bring them into being. It is only while they are still plans for the future that the development manager can apply himself to them in terms of all functions—distribution, production, conservation and personnel relations. Of these, the first three have already been discussed in their relation to development. It remains to discuss the last-named.

It is a weakness of some managements that too little attention is paid to depreciation and obsolescence as applied to human beings. It is well recognised that machines grow old, break down and ultimately reach the end of their useful lives and it is considered the essence of good management to make adequate provision against these eventualities. Little or no thought, however, is given to making provision for the ageing, break down and ultimate retirement of the personnel of the firm.

True, a pension scheme is often operated but this is a poor substitute for the sort of attention that ought to be paid to so vital a factor as man-power. No development manager will content himself with the thought that a generous pension scheme will solve the problems of the future—development problems—in their relation to personnel matters. A pension scheme is no more than a means of ensuring that the firm can carry out its moral obligations to care, in old age, for those who have given devoted service during their active years. It does not in any way meet the difficulties contingent on the inescapable fact that people do get older, do retire and do, on occasion, leave or die unexpectedly.

We have already seen that the principal job of the development manager is to apply research technique to the framing of future plans for his company. These plans embrace, in the main, expansion and the adoption of new methods and processes. It follows that such planning would be empty indeed if it failed to consider the human beings without whose agency the best of plans would be abortive.

As in the case of the other functions, the development manager is little concerned with people and things as they are in the present; he is, however, keenly interested in the sort, calibre, number and training of the people who will be available at the time when his plans mature. It will be too late, then, to think about recruiting new technicians, new executives and, possibly, new directors. The time to think of this is the present.

So the development manager has to look at his list of personnel and try to see each individual as he will be in five, ten or fifteen years' time—and he must include himself in this survey since he is no less human than his colleagues and fellow workers.

At first glance, some obvious facts emerge from such a list. It may well be that, in ten years' time, all the directors will have retired, as will many of the executives and key-men in the technical field. Ten years is not too long a period in which to prepare for such a decimation.

The list as it will appear five years hence is a guide to priorities. Here it may be that only half the Board will have retired, one of the senior executives and less than half the technical specialists.

Thinking first of those likely to retire first, the development manager must satisfy himself that, individually, there is someone in training and being groomed to succeed each when the date for retirement comes.

It is a matter of policy whether the persons being groomed for promotion are actually told the fact ; sometimes it is kinder to the senior personnel not to draw attention to the preparations being made to succeed them but, on grounds of good management, it is preferable that there should be no secret about it.

By working carefully through the list of personnel, the development manager will eventually satisfy himself that every foreseeable vacancy will have someone ready trained to fill it when it occurs and this will mean, of course, that the training and grooming scheme must embrace all the personnel. It would be little use training someone to take an executive's place if, when he came to be promoted, he himself left a vacancy that could not be readily filled.

It has been said that everyone on the ladder of management must be conscious of doing three jobs : the one he's paid for, learning the job of his next senior and teaching his own job to his next junior. This illustrates the framework within which a development manager must lay his plans.

Even when this is done he must go further; he must enquire whether, in the event of expansion or the introduction of new processes, the personnel as it will exist at the time will be adequate. Will there be enough people trained in the right jobs ? Will there be technicians able to handle new methods ? If not, who must be recruited, how and when must they be trained ?

Only by reasoning such as this can the development manager really be sure that his plans will work.

To sum up, there must be someone in every firm, large or small, whose job, or part of whose job, it is to live, mentally, in the future, to see the present organisation as transitional, to concern himself with all those many details which can be classed as part of development. In his sphere, he has an interest in all the functions of management. He must, since it is his task to supply the drawings for the firm of the future and no firm can develop other than by means of the functions of management.

The firm that ignores development doesn't just stand still ; it slips backwards.

It will have been noted that the work of the development manager is more technical than managerial. For this reason the term " development manager " is sometimes replaced by director of development—a title which more aptly describes his activities.

CHAPTER XVI

The Management of Stores

I propose to interpret the title of this chapter in its widest sense and bring within its scope all that part of management which has to do with materials. Largely, of course, I shall be discussing the routines and methods used in dealing with those responsible for materials. To discuss in detail problems peculiar to individual materials would, by definition, be a departure from the study of management.

The attitude of all those in a managerial capacity towards those dealing with materials and finished goods should be the same as their attitude towards those dealing with finance. The same care, precautions, safeguards and checks that are customary in the accounts department should, therefore, be applied to the handling, transport and consumption of materials ; materials are merely the company's money in another form.

Surprisingly often one hears quite complacent remarks about the difficulty of keeping accurate stores records, the incidence of petty pilfering of materials or discrepancies in stores balances. If anything like this occurred in the accounts department it would be a matter for consideration—and violent action—at Board level. It is, however, often considered as of minor significance if it occurs in terms of materials and if the losses and discrepancies are relatively small.

I have been told more than once that, as a cost accountant, I ought to realise that the cost of keeping a completely accurate check on vast quantities of small parts, such as screws, would be much greater than the amount lost through rough and ready record keeping. This may or may not be so, but I cannot believe that an accurate check on materials does not pay for itself in the long run, even though the return may take the intangible form of enhanced respect for honesty and accuracy that will be engendered throughout the organisation.

The first link between the company and the materials it buys is forged by the purchasing department. This may consist of a department in its own right with a staff of clerks operating under the control of a buyer ranking immediately below the managing director; or it may consist merely of a buying clerk working single-handed under the control of the works manager. The size and importance of the purchasing department will depend on the size of the organisation, on the diversity and quantity of materials customarily bought and on the nature of those materials.

Some materials can be bought by price list and their buying calls for no special knowledge. A buying clerk could handle these satisfactorily. In other cases materials may have to pass stringent technical tests or may be of such a nature that the state of the market must be foreseen by someone with a knowledge of the specific technicalities concerned. Here it may well be wiser to appoint a high-salaried official to do the purchasing and to give him a large measure of authority.

Whoever be responsible for purchasing, first intimation of requirements will reach him from the works manager. As the man responsible for consuming materials, he alone can be in a position to predict what he will need.

True, in the case of certain materials with a regular consumption rate the works manager may well place what is, in effect, a standing order under which the purchasing department is free to order this material at regular intervals but, even then, the authority is still vested in the works manager. If, through loss of a contract or some other cause, the call for the material diminished or ceased, information to this effect would have to be supplied by the works manager to the purchasing department.

The purchasing officer—I use the term to describe the individual placing orders with suppliers, whatever his managerial status—the purchasing officer, if he be worth his salt, aims to be very much more than a mere transmitter of orders from works manager to supplier. He should also be an adviser to his company on all matters of supply and should, in addition, be keenly interested in material control from the placing of the order until the material is issued to the factory for processing.

His job thus offers considerable scope and is capable of almost perpetual expansion. The organisation of his office should be constructed accordingly.

Perhaps the most important feature in his office will be a card index of actual and potential suppliers. The creation and maintenance of this index will call for a prolonged and continuous study of many trade periodicals circulating in all the trades in which the suppliers are interested.

From the advertisements and editorial references will be extracted the names, addresses and capabilities of all firms apparently in a position to satisfy the multifarious needs of the purchasing officer.

Having indexed these in detail under headings identifying various kinds of materials, the purchasing officer will next approach each firm in turn and solicit price lists, details of terms of business, approximate delivery dates and other relevant information. In many cases his enquiries will lead to a visit from a salesman from whom, possibly, an impression can be gained, later to be recorded, of the relevant firm's methods, standing and integrity.

Some details of these will be recorded on the card index. Where this is not possible, as in the case of price lists and catalogues, a separate library will be built up linked by cross-reference to the filing system.

The purchasing officer who possesses and keeps up to date such a comprehensive system will clearly be in a strong position should his regular supplier fail him or should he be faced with some sudden and unexpected demand for a seldom-handled material.

In selecting the supplier to be favoured with his orders, the purchasing officer will have many factors to consider.

Price, of course, is one; among the others are quality, service, delivery dates, reliability and capacity to supply in the quantities required.

When the purchasing officer is in the fortunate position of being able to place orders on a large scale, he will be wise to deal with several competing suppliers for each material. In this way, he can take advantage of competitive prices and protect his firm against such eventualities as fire, breakdown, strikes or accidents in a supplier's premises.

Even so, this policy must be followed with caution. Too wide a spread of orders will reduce their individual size to the point when they become unattractive to the suppliers and the purchasing officer can no longer command the attention and service given to a big customer. The aim is to be a big customer to a limited range of suppliers rather than a small customer to a wide range.

To continue with the description of the purchasing department organisation, provision must be made to record all orders placed and see that deliveries are made on the promised dates. For this purpose, copies of the actual orders can be filed and scanned daily, delivery details being noted on the backs. Alternatively, brief but adequate details of orders can be transferred to specially ruled cards, carrying spaces for delivery details and other comments.

For the rest, the purchasing department organisation will provide for the necessary typewriting and for the checking of all invoices against orders. Only when certified as correct by the purchasing department will invoices be accepted by the accounts department for payment.

It has already been explained that instructions to purchase will originate with the works manager. From what has been said since, it will be clear that additional information relating to deliveries will also be needed in the purchasing department. This comes from the stores at which, usually, deliveries are made.

The chief storekeeper, then, must maintain close liaison with the purchasing department. He will almost certainly fall under the authority of the works manager but will work closely with the purchasing officer irrespective of the origin of this latter's authority.

When an order is passed to a supplier, details of goods ordered and promised delivery dates should be made available to the chief storekeeper. He thus knows what to expect and when to expect it and is consequently able to allocate space in advance.

When a delivery is made, the quantity delivered is checked against the delivery note, if possible in the presence of the delivery agent or, if not, as soon as possible afterwards. It is this checking that is so often cursorily undertaken and which I have suggested should receive a maximum of care.

It is not sufficient to accept and store a hundred boxes of parts, for instance, without opening at least two or three immediately and confirming that they hold the right parts in the right quantities. Later, all should be opened and checked in the same way.

In the case of very small, very numerous and inexpensive parts, such as screws or rivets, there is a good argument against an actual count; there is no argument, though, against a weight-check of each box, sack or other container.

Some materials purchased may be of so complex a nature that the chief storekeeper is not qualified to accept them. In these cases a technical inspection must be carried out at the earliest convenient moment by someone competent to assess the quality of the consignment.

When the chief storekeeper, aided where necessary by technical assistance, is satisfied that he has received in good condition the materials which are the subject of the delivery note, he should initial this document and pass it through to the purchasing department, where it will be accepted as evidence of delivery of the materials listed on it.

Having passed on the delivery note, the chief storekeeper takes the goods into stores and sees that they are entered in stores records.

The physical taking of goods into stores presents few

problems other than those of capacity, though, of course, care must be taken to see that goods for immediate use are accessible and not stacked under or behind goods likely to remain in stores for some considerable while. This is only common sense.

Stores records need not—indeed should not—be complicated. For most purposes a perpetual inventory system is quite adequate linked, if required, with bin cards.

Under the perpetual inventory system a card is made out for each kind of material in stores. At the head the card shows the kind of material, the supplier's name, its location in stores and the maximum and minimum levels within which the quantity in stock is to be kept.

Below this heading, the card is ruled in columns to carry entries indicating delivery note number, quantity delivered, requisition number, quantity requisitioned and outstanding balance. The necessary date columns are also included.

These cards are made up daily from delivery notes and requisitions, the balance being extended after each movement. A clerk can do this work and by means of the maximum and minimum permitted levels can ensure, without reference elsewhere, that adequate but not excessive supplies are available. Only when the balance in hand is above or below permitted limits need the storekeeper's attention be attracted.

It is true that the settling and occasional revision of the permitted levels for each item of stock call for considerable care. These levels will usually be set by the purchasing officer, the works manager and the storekeeper in concert. Factors to be taken into account will be, in the case of each item, average time lag between order and delivery, consumption rate, perishability, likelihood of obsolescence and available storage capacity.

Normally, the maximum level will never be exceeded since over-ordering can only arise from some administrative failure. When, however, the storekeeper's attention is drawn to a decrease in stock below the permitted minimum, he will notify the works manager accordingly. This latter can then transmit an instruction to the purchasing officer to place a further order for the items concerned.

In a great many cases where a perpetual inventory is properly worked, bin cards can be abolished. At best a bin card is little more than an additional check on balance in hand. It consists of a card attached to the bin, rack or storage receptacle of each item in stock. Intakes and out-goings are noted on the bin card as they occur, so that in theory the balance shown by the bin card should agree both with the actual quantity in stock and with the perpetual inventory cards.

By making a point of checking physically one or two items selected at random at frequent intervals throughout the year and comparing the actual quantity in stock with the perpetual inventory balance, a great deal of arduous and expensive overtime can be dispensed with at stocktaking time.

Where a production control department is in existence, a duplicate set of inventory cards is often kept there. These cards are made up from the same original documents—delivery notes and requisitions—which are routed through the department after they leave the stores on the way to the purchasing department and cost office respectively. This duplicate record not only enables the production controller to have a complete picture of materials available, it also serves as a useful check against the inventory in use in the stores.

It will be the duty primarily of the works manager, but also of the purchasing officer, to see that the variety of types of material is kept to a minimum. In this way the purchasing officer can place a few large orders in place of many small ones, thereby enjoying better terms, the storekeeper's problems are simplified, record keeping is reduced and many potential mistakes eliminated in advance. Every attempt should be made, therefore, to standardise on materials wherever possible. This may mean bringing pressure to bear on the design staff and may call for a high degree of educational ability in the works manager but it will pay handsomely if it be substantially achieved.

Little can usefully be said here about the actual layout

of the stores since this is a matter inextricably bound up with the space available, the nature of the materials handled, the quantity and consumption rate of each and the value and perishability of individual items. Suffice it to say that accessibility should be the key-note coupled with a numbering or other system by means of which individual items can be located readily even in the absence of the man who ought to know. Perhaps the real solution of stores layout problems lies in securing the services of a competent and experienced storekeeper and in giving him a free hand to lay the stores out in his own way. Such a man is worth a great deal of any company's money. He may well be responsible for many thousands of pounds worth of materials.

Since materials find a place in all production and since materials enter production from stores, it follows that there must be liaison between stores and cost office where information about materials is needed in connection with every job.

This liaison can most simply be maintained by passing requisitions from stores to cost office daily. The requisition will carry the number of the job for which the material is needed, the quantity issued and the signature of the requisitioning foreman ; it is unlikely, though, to carry the price since it is scarcely the duty of the storekeeper to price his issues.

The price, then, must be added to the requisition before it is of any use in the cost office. The addition can be made either from a price list kept in the cost office or from one kept in the production control department if the requisition be routed through it.

In the cost office the priced requisitions provide the materials entries for the cost sheets and, later, form the basic information for materials summaries and other statistical analyses.

CHAPTER XVII

The Human Element—1

Mention has already been made earlier of the fact that, since management is the art of directing human activities, it is not strictly possible to consider the human element as distinct from every function of management. Nevertheless, a large proportion of human element matters is capable of being separated and placed in the care of a specialist or functional department.

Thus it is that a personnel department can find plenty to occupy its time without attempting to remove from each individual manager his own responsibility for his staff in their capacity as human beings.

To this extent—that its function is all-pervasive—the personnel department differs from the other functional departments. The sales office, the accounts department, the production function and the development function all operate within clear-cut limits. Liaison between them and co-operation there must be, but this can be carried out in accordance with an established routine.

The personnel department, however, exercises something of a watching brief over the entire personnel. Without in any way actively interfering in the internal operation of any department, it is nevertheless always at hand to advise, help or deal with difficulties of a human nature basis wherever these arise.

In addition to this advisory capacity, the personnel department also deals in its own right with a multitude of more mundane matters essential to the well-being of the employee but clearly not the responsibility of individual department managers. It is these matters which are to be discussed in this and the succeeding chapter. Reference will be made frequently to the personnel manager and a definition will be helpful, especially to those whose firms have not yet set up fully-fledged personnel departments.

By personnel manager is implied any individual in any firm who has as his especial care the well-being of the employees. It matters not whether he be styled personnel manager or whether he be the works manager or one of the directors. Someone must have the employees' welfare at heart and for the present purpose he is the personnel manager.

Clearly, if he is to do his duty effectively, he must be allowed to take a large share in the framing of personnel policy. After all, he is to carry out the policy and, further, he knows—or should make it his job to know—the particular and peculiar needs of the flock for which he is to care.

Even though he should have a hand in framing policy there is a good argument against his being a director of the company. For good or ill, directors are looked upon by employees as members of the " they " group ; " they " are the often anonymous arbiters of what shall be done ; " they ", it is all too often felt, are inflexibly opposed in principle and opinion to the " we " group of which employees see themselves as members.

It would be inappropriate in a book of this nature to examine the possible justification for this characteristic of the thought process of employees. It should not exist ; there should be no grounds for it and its eradication will be a principal plank in personnel policy. The personnel manager will be assisted in this educative pursuit if he himself is not a director ; if, in other words, he can rank as one of the " we " group.

This is not to say that there should not be a director charged with specialist—as opposed to general—care of the employees' well-being. Where, however, there is such a director he will be well advised to appoint a personnel manager between himself and the employees unless he is sufficiently fortunate to direct a firm where this misconception has already been abolished.

A personnel director will, by virtue of his seat on the

Board, have a big say in personnel policy. A personnel manager must be given an equivalent voice even though he be an employee without director's status.

In framing policy the Board will consider all the eventualities likely to arise in its relations with its employees and will lay down in advance the framework or broad lines of action to be taken when, and if, each arises. It is a mistake to include in policy only the potential causes of large-scale trouble. Few troubles reach large proportions unless, in the first instance, small beginnings have been neglected. What may seem a trifling matter at Board level may well be a matter of major consequence to the man on the factory floor or office worker whom it closely concerns.

Policy will thus embrace the Board's attitude to absenteeism, voluntary and involuntary, joint consultation, trade union negotiations, discipline, promotion, transfer, retirement, remuneration, suggestion schemes, social amenities, canteen services, medical attention and training to mention at random but a few of the subject headings which will guide discussion.

With a policy in existence, the personnel manager has a directive to guide him in the vast majority of the problems that will confront him and in the decisions he will be called on to make. By following this directive consistently he will ensure not only that justice is done but also that justice is seen to be done. On this, perhaps, morale depends more than on any other single factor.

Like all policies, the personnel policy will not remain static. Like the business itself, it will become out-dated and diminishingly effective unless it be developed as time goes by. An excellent and enlightened personnel policy of ten years ago, for instance, might well be regarded as quite inadequate in the industrial conditions prevailing to-day.

This development of policy must take place in step with the apparent need for it and in accordance with progressive thought, indications of which will probably come first from the employees themselves. The Board must not be too aloof to consider carefully all such indications and, where appropriate, to amplify them and give expression to them by broadening policy.

Means, therefore, must be provided whereby the feelings, needs and attitudes of employees can be brought in an orderly manner to the attention of the Board. The larger the organisation, the greater the gulf between the Board and the employees and, therefore, the greater the need for such a channel of information.

A competent personnel manager, of course, will have developed his own sixth sense to tell him a great deal of what is being thought and felt by the employees. He will, too, have the advantage of direct man-to-man contact with them. Even so, this is but a partial solution of the problem inherent in achieving a free flow of information on personnel matters between lowest and highest levels.

The most effective way in which management can transmit and receive a regular flow of fresh information is by the constitution and support of a democratically elected joint-consultative body, truly representative of all grades of employee. The setting up and working of such a body are not nearly such easy tasks as they may seem.

The joint consultative body may be a works council, charged merely with the maintenance of good industrial relations ; alternatively it may be a joint production council with wider terms of reference embracing technical matters peculiar to the company's production methods. In this latter case there may be a sub-committee to deal with industrial relations.

The precise terms of reference of the body, however, are matters of domestic concern in individual cases and, as such, are not suitable for discussion here. They are, too, of much less importance than the working of the body itself.

All too often works councils, set up in all good faith by enlightened managements and supported enthusiastically in their early stages by the employer—all too often such councils have, within a matter of months, deteriorated into little more than platforms for the airing of grievances and complaints about canteen food and sanitary arrangements.

It may be argued that a means for giving vent to complaints is, itself, a worth-while cause on the ground that it prevents frustration. This may be to some extent true but no one who has seen a works council functioning really well would ever be satisfied with the stultified imitation that has been described.

There are, then, certain prerequisites to the setting up of a works council likely to perform its tasks adequately. The first of these prerequisites is undoubtedly mutual confidence between higher management and employees. Each must feel that the other is coming to the council table fully determined to deal sincerely with all matters raised. There must be no hint of the managerial attitude, too frequently found, that the employees' grievances can always be talked out or skated over if management be dominant enough. At the council table all are equal and, by hypothesis, all have at heart the improvement of industrial relations in the interest of the firm.

A second prerequisite to a successful council is the assurance of just and fair representation. The scheme of balloting for representatives must, therefore, recognise that even within a small department there are workers of different status and, for this reason, different problems. It is, therefore, unsatisfactory to elect representatives on a " per department or factory " basis. Rather should the representation be on a " per grade or status " basis.

For example, in a firm embracing nine factories of some hundred employees in each, it would be unsatisfactory to elect two representatives per factory and leave it at that. Success would be unlikely.

A much better method would be the election of representatives from the foremen, chargehands, skilled technicians, apprentices, service hands, stores personnel and office staff. In this way each grade of employee is assured of a representative versed in his own peculiar difficulties.

So much for employee representation.

The management, too, will, of course, be represented at the council. This is best achieved by the nomination of one or more senior executives with the right to co-opt others when specific problems are being debated.

The third prerequisite is a clearly written and well-defined document setting out the terms of reference and stating in unequivocal words the subjects which may and may not be discussed. Again, the actual subjects permitted and banned are less important than is the need clearly to state them.

By way of example, it is usual to exclude as topics for discussion such matters as individual salaries, as this would be invidious, and wage scales as, usually, these are subject to trade union or wages council negotiations. Some firms, too, would exclude discussion of company finances ; others would welcome the opportunity to acquaint employees with a detailed analysis of the company's accounts.

The council so constituted will need chairman and secretary. These can be permanent officials if desired but, in the interests of confidence, it is as well to appoint the managing director as nominal chairman and, in practice, to let the chair alternate between two vice-chairmen appointed from the management and the employees respectively. Similarly, the personnel manager is probably best suited to act as joint secretary supported by one of the employees. Given an arrangement of this nature and assured of whole-hearted enthusiasm on the part of all concerned, a works council will at least stand a fair chance of meeting with success.

Acting as joint secretary of the works council is, however, but one of the many duties a personnel manager will have to perform if he is to be true to his profession and his firm.

He will have a predominant voice in the recruiting, posting, training, promotion and eventual retirement of the personnel of his firm. To what extent he will exercise his authority at different executive levels depends on his position in the management hierarchy and on the policy of his company. Despite this, however, a considerable amount of time will be absorbed.

It should, perhaps, be explained here that the personnel manager does not, in any sense, usurp the privileges of managers and department heads to select those with whom they wish to work. Rather is the personnel manager's function an advisory one.

By hypothesis, he is the executive presumed to be trained and knowledgeable in interviewing techniques, training schemes, aptitude tests and like matters relative to employees as individuals. It is natural, therefore, that he should be required to place this training and knowledge at the disposal of his colleagues and his firm when needed.

In the case of a new employee, therefore, the personnel manager will be notified of the vacancy and will use his knowledge of sources of supply to secure a number of applicants. These he will interview and grade, from his experience, into probables, possibles and those quite unsuitable for the vacancy to be filled. He will then draw up a short list of candidates whom he, himself, feels to be adequate to fill the vacancy and submit it, with his own recommendations, to the manager of the department where the vacancy has occurred. The manager need not accept the personnel manager's recommendation, nor need he agree to accept any of the short-listed candidates but, since the personnel manager is a specialist in his own field, it is usually unwise to ignore his skilled advice.

The applicants short-listed are interviewed again by the responsible manager who has the comforting knowledge that all on the list have already been approved by his expert colleague as suitable for the job. He is thus free to select the most congenial applicant without bothering his head about aptitude or abilities.

A similar process attends training and promotion. The personnel manager advises his management on the drawing up of a comprehensive training syllabus. When this is agreed, the personnel manager brings it into being, supervises it and keeps records of attendances, test results and the like. He does not possess the authority to demand the participation of any other manager's staff, though the managing director may insist that all do attend.

In the matter of promotion, either the personnel manager selects a junior ripe for promotion or a vacancy is notified to him into which he feels a junior could be promoted. In either case it is a matter of negotiation between the personnel manager on the one hand and, on the other, the manager of the junior and the manager with the vacancy.

In a well-founded firm little difficulty is usually experienced in reaching friendly agreement but much will depend on the personnel manager's approach. This should be a tactful one implying that the promotion is in the interest alike of the junior concerned and the firm. Should there be difficulty, however, the managing director must be called on to arbitrate as in the case of all disputes between specialist executives.

Similarly, the right to discharge still remains in the hands of individual managers though the personnel manager usually has the unwelcome job of conveying the information to the victim.

The fact that a certain employee is no longer required is notified to the personnel manager who ascertains the reason and examines his records of the employee's career with the firm. If, as often happens, the grounds are redundancy and the employee has a good record, the personnel manager will make every effort to transfer the employee into another department. He is, indeed, required to make this attempt by the terms of the Redundancy Payments Act, 1965. Apart from that, a good employee versed in the firm's methods and ways is always more valuable than a newcomer.

Only if a transfer proves impossible will the personnel manager interview the employee and discharge him, at the same time giving him any help he can towards finding other employment.

Exceptions to this procedure are instant discharges for insubordination. Clearly, if a foreman be grossly insulted by an employee, he must have an inalienable right to discharge the man on the spot. Even the Essential Works Order during the war recognised and preserved this right.

When insubordination occurs, then, the foreman or manager can, if he see fit, discharge the offender without reference to the personnel manager but he must report the full facts of the case at the earliest possible moment, prefer-ably in writing.

If the personnel manager finds that one manager or foreman is using this method of discharge too frequently, he will interview him and enquire more deeply into the reasons for so much apparent insubordination. He may also offer a word or two of advice. If, even after this, dis-charges for insubordination continue to be made by the same man to a disproportionate extent the only action for the personnel manager is to have a talk with the offender's superior or, in extreme cases, to send a confidential note to the managing director.

The personnel manager, by virtue of his office, can never be fully identified with management or employees. He stands, as it were, midway between both parties endeavouring always to weld them into one common unit all working for the betterment of the firm of which the prosperity is of personal benefit to everyone.

This aspect of his work is particularly marked in his responsibility for seeing that the provisions of the Factories Acts and other industrial regulations are fully observed. It may often be that, in his tours of the factory, he will note some infringement of, for example, a safety provision.

Irrespective of what it may cost to comply with the Act, the personnel manager must insist that the necessary guard, or whatever be necessary, be made available. Here he is acting in the interests of the employees to the apparent detriment of the management though, of course, this is not so. It can, in the end, benefit no management to have unsafe conditions in its factory.

It often happens, too, that a complaint by an employee against the management is found, after careful sifting by the personnel manager, to be justified in substance. Here, too, the personnel manager will advise the management to rectify the trouble ; he will, in fact, side with the employee against his own management.

A management wise enough to have appointed a personnel manager will not see anything unusual in this apparent anomaly and will, in nearly every case, accept the personnel manager's advice.

If the advice is not accepted, if the employee's grievance is not righted, it would seem that the only course open to the personnel manager would be to resign. His position would be intolerable and, as a professional man, he would have no option in the matter.

The further duties of the personnel manager in his capacity as custodian of the employees as human beings include, of course, the provision and supervision of welfare facilities, first-aid rooms, canteens and social clubs. He will also be available to give—or secure—advice on a host of employees' problems.

Time so spent is not wasted either on humanitarian or more mundane grounds. A neglected employee or one with a problem on his mind is only partly effective and if, with his greater knowledge, experience and contacts, the personnel manager can make him happier or more contented he is, by the same token, restoring to full stature an erstwhile handicapped employee.

In this chapter I have dealt with the personnel manager's activities in broad outline. In the next, I propose to cover some of the same ground, sketching in some of the detail.

Remember that the personnel manager's function differs in two ways from that of his colleagues, the executives responsible for other functional departments. First, the personnel function is all-pervasive and is not limited in scope to any one department; it operates wherever the human element be found. Secondly, the personnel manager may, on occasion, be called on to take sides against his own management in the interest of the employees. Tact, therefore, coupled with deep human sympathies and interests must be among his principal attributes.

CHAPTER XVIII

The Human Element—2

In this chapter I am proposing to deal less with personnel policy and all the considerations that surround it and rather more with the application of that policy to those whom it concerns. That is, to everyone employed.

It must be realised, in this connection, that there is a big difference between framing a policy and applying it to individuals each of whom, in terms of human nature, is different in some respects from his fellows and each of whom, for that reason, is likely to react differently. Policy, in short, must be capable of detailed adaptation to human nature since human nature cannot be adapted to fit a given policy.

This is not to say, though, that so much latitude should be given that the policy itself becomes an academic ideal never, in fact, to be attained. Rather is it to say that the policy of the management to the personnel should be one of human understanding and should contain within it provision for modification within limits when such modification seems desirable.

By way of example, it would be wrong to base a rigid policy on the conception that management's only duty to its employees lay in paying adequate and just wages or salaries at regular intervals. This, it is true, is one of management's obligations but, rigidly applied, it can only induce a soulless and barren relationship.

Some employee may be the victim of domestic trouble which, admittedly, is not the fault of the management. But if a loan of a few pounds would help him, wise policy would permit of such a loan being granted with, of course, proper provision for repayment. In short, any policy that envisages an employee as no more than a number on the clock is a bad policy. It must never be forgotten that the youngest junior has his hopes, fears, ambitions, interests and troubles no less than has every member of the Board of directors.

Even if this evident fact be forgotten by the Board of directors, it is the job of the personnel manager to keep it in mind at all times. For that reason, the personnel manager should be given considerable freedom of action in following the policy laid down by the Board and, of course, himself. He should also be kept constantly informed of what his colleagues are doing.

In the matter of staff salaries, particularly, it will be necessary clearly to define the advisory relationship which must be established between the personnel manager and the heads of other departments. Clearly, it could create an impossible situation if the personnel manager were to be the only person authorised to settle individual salaries and wages, if any employee seeking an increase were compelled to do so from someone other than the head of his own department.

Conversely, an almost equally impossible situation would be created if each department head were free to settle salaries, wages and increases without reference to the rates and scales paid by his colleagues.

To integrate these two extremes, policy should set the scales to which salaries should be related and, in the factory, policy should lay down the method of payment. It would then become the function of the personnel manager, or custodian of personnel policy, to see that these scales and methods are observed by all and that strict justice is maintained between all employees, whatever their departments or duties. This function he will perform by requiring all rates of pay and proposed increases to be notified to him before being granted, retaining to himself the right to suggest modification or adjustments where, in his opinion, these seem desirable in the interests of harmony.

Bear in mind that the personnel manager should not reserve to himself the right to over-ride his colleagues. His right is limited to one of suggestion, and explanation. In the event that his colleagues dispute his argument or decline to accept his suggestions, then the managing director must assume the final responsibility of arbitrating in the dispute.

This is quite simple really, but regrettably often this delicate balance is either ignored or, if established, is not maintained. Then, it's only a matter of time before the whole executive structure disintegrates.

I now turn to the human element problem that attends the engagement of new workers. The personnel manager, it has already been explained, has the responsibility for selecting a short list of capable applicants, leaving the final selection to the head of the appropriate department. It will be seen that, in order to perform his part with a reasonable chance of success, the personnel manager must be provided with full details of the sort of job which has to be filled.

In a small firm, it may be sufficient to advise the personnel manager that a compositor, an office junior, a book-keeper or a junior clerk is needed. With a close knowledge of all jobs, acquired by personal observation, the personnel manager may be adequately informed. Not so, however, in a large factory with a multitudinous selection of jobs, each requiring special skills, aptitudes, abilities and physiques.

In such cases it is customary to analyse the job and to reduce the analysis to a job specification.

Job analysis is not an easily undertaken task. It consists of writing down, in the most precise detail, exactly how a job is done. When finished, it should, in theory, be possible for any intelligent person, quite untutored in the job, to pick up the job analysis card and perform the job correctly. The difficulties of job analysis can be more clearly appreciated if one tries to write down the full sequence of operations involved in, for example, changing a light bulb, threading a needle or adjusting a lavatory cistern. These are relatively simple domestic jobs, far less complex than many in a factory.

For this reason job analysis can only be undertaken by a highly-skilled and trained member of the staff. It will take him a long time but, at the end of it, he will have an analysis card for every job in the organisation and, arising out of his work, there will have been established a standard method of performing each job. If, therefore, the analysis be taken after due regard has been paid to motion study, the standard will represent the best possible method under existing conditions. New employees will then be taught the correct way, wherever they be set to work and whoever is responsible for the tuition. This, alone, is a most valuable feature of job analysis.

The analyses, though, are not only useful in this way; they become, in addition, the bases of job specifications.

Briefly, a job specification is a statement of all the qualities required for the performance of the task. Thus, individual jobs require physical strength, intelligence, good colour vision, pliant fingers, an ability to endure monotony, mathematical aptitude and many other like qualities. By relating these to the job analysis, a job specification can be prepared which will give the personnel manager a clear guide as to what he must look for in interviewing applicants.

The job specifications should be drawn up by several persons in committee. The personnel manager should be there, the works manager, the appropriate foreman or charge-hand and, if there be one, the works doctor. On occasion, too, reference might well be made to the man performing the job.

The net result of all this is that there is available a set of job analysis cards giving full instructions for the performance of each job and, keyed to these, a set of job specification cards listing the personal qualities required for the performance of each job. The routine, thereafter, is simple.

When a vacancy occurs it is only necessary to advise the personnel department of the fact and refer to the job concerned. With this information, the personnel manager can turn up the relevant specification and at once see exactly the sort of applicant likely to suit.

So much for individual employees. We must now consider the employees as a group with, of course, all those characteristics that differentiate the group-mind from the individual mind. A great many of management's rules and edicts will, of their nature, impinge on the group, as opposed to the individual ; they must, therefore, be considered in terms of the group-mind.

The theory has long been exploded that it is sufficient for management to give instructions and for employees to carry them out. There may have been a time when this procedure worked but, in these enlightened days, one wonders whether it ever worked to the advantage of anybody.

To-day, employees are considered to have minds and to be possessed of intelligence. Further, management realises that that intelligence can be turned to the advantage of all if it be canalised in the right direction. An intelligent employee will use his intelligence anyway ; nothing can stop him. He may use it in a way detrimental to his company's interests or, if he is aware of all the facts relating to his job, he may use it to further his company's interests. It is better, therefore, to consult with an employee than to keep him completely in the dark as to the reason for, and purpose behind, the work he is doing. In terms of the group-mind, this is achieved by joint consultation.

This has been discussed in some detail in the preceding chapter ; one or two additional notes will, therefore, suffice to round off the subject.

The minutes of each meeting should, after approval by the chairman, be circulated to all employees so that they can see to what extent their own views have been aired by their representatives. In this way a substantial measure of confidence is engendered and much of the worker's suspicion of the management can be removed.

How often meetings shall be held and whether they be held in working hours or not are matters for domestic arrangement and no hard and fast rules can be cited. Provision should, however, be made for calling the council together on a signed request, stating the reason, from a given number of employees.

Naturally, there will be much negotiation that does not fall within the powers of a works council. Trade union negotiation, for example, can only be handled by the personnel manager and works manager though the council should be kept advised of the progress of such negotiation and be allowed to comment thereon.

Another duty falling to the personnel manager is the handling of suggestion schemes, some of which have proved valuable aids to management ; others, usually through mis-handling, have proved useless.

Suggestion schemes are intended to give effect to the belief that the man on the bench, actually performing a task, is well fitted to suggest ways of simplifying or speeding up that task. Unless there be some channel by which he can put his ideas forward and unless there be some prospect of reward for so doing, many a man will keep his ideas to himself.

By providing boxes in various parts of the factory into which suggestion-slips can be put, the management aims to tap this source of potentially improved efficiency. Employees are notified that a reward will be paid for all suggestions accepted.

Naturally many unusable suggestions will be put forward, some fatuous, some technically impossible, some facetious but, among them, there may well be some containing the germ of a practical idea.

The golden rules, which a personnel manager will have to adopt if the scheme is to be successful, are these.

The boxes must be opened regularly and frequently by someone of standing in the organisation. All suggestions must be considered seriously and, where unworkable, the reason must be explained to the employee concerned. As short a time as possible must be allowed to elapse between the opening of the boxes and notifications to employees. Rewards should be generous and even given, on occasion, for unacceptable suggestions where these show intelligence and conscientious thought in the management's interests. Provision, in the terms of the scheme, must be made for dealing fairly with possible patents arising from suggestions.

The personnel manager's duties so far listed do not, by any

means, constitute his entire obligations to the human element of industrial life. He has still to think daily of his flock as individuals.

In this respect, there will be a thousand and one ways in which he can be of assistance and can help to foster that confidence and loyalty which is the mark of a firm with a good personnel policy and a good personnel manager. Generally, this part of his job is called employee services, a broad term which cloaks probably the most interesting part of personnel work.

Starting from the incontrovertible assumption that the value of an employee to his firm is enhanced beyond measure if he be happy, contented and loyal, the employee services rendered by the personnel manager have as their object the achievement of this state in all employees.

Strictly speaking, it is no concern of the management if an employee's wife has left him, if he is being sued for debt, if his landlord is bringing pressure to bear on him or if his daughter is wayward. On the other hand, an employee suffering from these or any other home worries is, to that extent, a sub-standard worker.

The personnel manager, therefore, invites confidential chats at which these troubles can be disclosed. The mere opportunity to talk is, itself, a big relief to most employees but, beyond that, it often happens that the personnel manager, with his wider experience, can help actively. In this connection, the personnel manager must be willing and able to call, if he sees fit, on any of a number of sources of expert help which can be placed at the disposal of the troubled employee. The personnel manager may refer him to a lawyer; he may commend him to the attention of his parish Priest, Minister or Rabbi; he may enlist the help of one of the many charitable organisations; he may ring up the local welfare authorities to seek their help. If the personnel manager is sympathetic, understanding and wise in the ways of the world, he will be able, in very many cases, to be the means of restoring the troubled employee to happiness and peace of mind.

Finally, but not exhaustively, in his care for the human element, the personnel manager will take an active interest in the social side of factory life. He will inspire sports activities, social evenings, dances, outings and competitions, trying all the time to make the factory less a mere work-place than one where employees can develop a wider social life and social conscience than is possible in their home surroundings.

After all, an employee spends a very large part of his life within the factory gates.

CHAPTER XIX

The Principles of Management

During the course of this book, mention has been made to scientific management. This is a common designation in management, so common, in fact, that there is grave danger of misunderstanding. Is management a science ? Probably not yet, possibly it never will be wholly scientific in conception. Nevertheless, there is sufficient science in management to justify calling it scientific management.

A science, according to the dictionary, is an organised body of knowledge accumulated on a subject and admitting of quantitative treatment ; it will be seen that management, as we know it, is only partly an organised body of knowledge and is only partly capable of quantitative treatment. It is certain that the body of knowledge will grow and will become increasingly subject to organisation; it is not so certain that management will ever be subject to wholly quantitative treatment. We have always to reckon with the human element.

Even so, no organised body of knowledge can exist, let alone develop, unless there be certain principles which can be established as, so to speak, fixed points to which to relate theory and practice as the scientific studies go forward. Without such principles there might be a body of knowledge, but it would not be an organised body. For example, an office might be able to operate without any past records but anyone taking it over would have to start without the benefit of any of the experience of his precursor.

By means of the principles of management so far evolved, the management thinking of each new brain can be co-ordinated to the thinking of others and the total body of knowledge thus accumulated can be organised for the good of all, including those yet to turn their attention to management.

There is, unfortunately, inadequate space in a book of this nature to give credit to all those great names which, in the past, have enhanced the pages of management literature. Three, though, must be mentioned.

F. W. Taylor, an American, is the man to whom is credited the first realisation that management had within it the elements of a science. He knew, from his practical engineering experience, that work at the bench was capable of measurement. He found that a detailed study of that work was amply repaid in terms of greater output per worker. He found, too, that intricate jobs could be broken down in such a way that workers could be taught to specialise in small parts of the whole job, thereby becoming more proficient, learning more quickly and, as a result, becoming more productive. This is known as division of labour. This book, for instance, was produced by specialist compositors, specialist machine minders, specialist folders, stitchers and bookbinders. Had it been produced by a number of versatile jacks-of-all-trades —even if they were capable of learning all trades—it is doubtful whether it would be as well made or as cheap as it is. Quantity production is only possible where labour can be divided into specialist units.

Henri Fayol, a French mining engineer, was among those who applied Taylor's ideas and developed from them certain principles of management, many of which are as true to-day as they were when they were published many decades ago. Fayol, though, tended to envisage management as a static science.

It remained for Mary Parker Follett, another American, to see management as a dynamic, constantly developing, science. She it was who postulated the Law of the Situation by which management was seen to be a series of changing situations each dependent on, and conditioned by, the preceding one. It is the Law of the Situation, argued Mary Parker Follett, which governs action by management and workers alike. Orders, therefore, should not be given "because I say so and because I'm the boss " but " because the situation demands this joint activity ".

Before passing on to the principles of management so far evolved, it is necessary to point out once again that management is a developing science and, for that reason, no set of principles can be regarded as static. Management, in its present stage, must be constantly seeking further bases of quantitative analysis, nothing must be accepted just because it has always been accepted in the past. New methods of measurement must be sought, tested, checked and passed into common management practice. We have already seen a great deal done in this direction—motion and time study, job analysis, cost control, the use of computers—but more remains to be done. Let this be remembered. Perhaps a short way of summarising what I have written so far in this chapter would be to say that scientific management is partly an art, or human skill, and partly a science to the extent that it is capable of being measured and reduced to principles which can, themselves, be taught to and expanded by future thinkers on the subject. Whether the part that is art will ever become scientific is not a prediction that I feel justified in making.

The first principle of management, then, is that there must be an objective ; management must know where it is going and how it is going to get there. This may seem obvious but a little thought will show that in many firms it is largely ignored. True, no management is ignorant of what it is making and selling, no management comes into being without such knowledge—but a surprising number of firms have no policy capable of being written down in clear and unequivocal terms. The managements of such firms know roughly where they are going but they appear to be relying on the tides and winds of fate to get them there. A policy is merely a statement of all the methods which the management proposes in order to achieve the objective implicit in its mere existence. It follows that the principle of the objective is being inadequately observed unless there exists a policy. No sane man would put to sea from, say, Liverpool for New York if his ideas of how to get there were as hazy as some of the vague generalisations that pass, in many cases, for statements of policy in the business world.

In amplification of the principle of the objective, it may be added that the objective, included in the policy, should be commonly accepted by all those, including workers, whose efforts will be required to achieve it. Neglect of this rapidly leads to divergence of interest between management and workers with consequent nullification of much of the efforts of all. If two horses pull a cart, their maximum effort can only be made when they both pull in the same direction ; any separation of their ways must reduce the individual effort of each until complete stagnation is reached when both pull opposite ways.

Let us, then, call this first principle that of the common objective.

Obviously, where there is a common objective, there must be leadership ; and the principle of leadership calls for some discussion.

By the nature of things, the original objective must be decided by the management. It is the management which brings the firm into being and it is the management which decides the purpose for so doing. If, as is no doubt always the case, the management is convinced that its objective is a sound one, then it is for management to convince the workers and enlist their support so as to make it a common objective.

To a large extent this can be done by frankness, fair dealing and consultation combined under the heading of education but if the objective is at all times to remain the common goal of all, leadership will have to play a very large part.

It is appropriate at this point to draw attention to the fact that some of the principles of management apply only to higher management—in this category is the principle of the common objective—while others apply at all levels where management is practised—that is, right down to the lowest ranking individual who includes within his job any direction of the activities of others. Leadership is one of these principles. Leadership at a high level must be such that similar qualities of leadership are inspired at all levels.

Some thinkers split the principle of leadership and introduce a principle of common thought. I feel though, that the ability to induce like thinking is of the very essence of leadership and that a principle of common thought is inherent in the two principles I have named.

Now, in order to give effect to the common objective, it will clearly be necessary for those at a high level to delegate their authority to, and to make responsible to them, all those who perform any management activity. In early days, this was loosely observed and consisted of little more than giving odd bits of the job of management to junior people to carry out. Now, however, Taylor's division of labour has been applied to management and it has been found vastly more satisfactory to break down the main job of management into various specialist parts—already discussed as functions—and to make various individuals responsible for functions and parts of functions instead of for a heterogeneous litter of jobs. Thus the delegation of responsibility and authority to specialists in the various functions is called the principle of functionalisation.

It would be of little use making functional chiefs responsible for the functions of management and giving them authority unless attention were paid to the manner in which those functional chiefs carried out their tasks. If no such attention were paid, it is possible that chaos might merely be removed to a lower stratum of the management hierarchy. Thus has evolved the principle of the span of control.

The basis of this principle is empirical. There is no mathematical formula to prove it. It has merely been found, over many years, that the capacity of one man to take responsibility for the actions and reports of others is limited to five, or at the most six, such subordinates. If a man be given more than this number of senior subordinates, each reporting to him and deriving their authority directly from him, he will be unable to do his own job of management adequately. Instead, he will become merely a harassed go-between always a long way behind events.

There may, of course, be men who can exceed six principal subordinates and still keep control of the situation but they are few. There are, too, occasions when this span of control can be exceeded but they are limited to those at the lower end of the management scale who, by definition, have only a small ingredient of management in their jobs.

These exceptions, then, do not destroy the validity of the principle of the span of control and any manager who finds himself directly responsible for the activities of more than five subordinates must very carefully examine his position. He will probably find that he has little time for doing his own job and that, instead, he is becoming more and more a confidant and transmitter of information for his subordinates. His solution is not difficult. He must so arrange that one or more of his present direct subordinates comes under the authority of another and no longer derives direct authority from the manager. By thus grouping his subordinates he will be able to reduce them within the scope of the principle of the span of control.

The next principle to be discussed is the very important one of co-ordination or producing the right results at the right time in the right way. The real truth of this principle can best be appreciated by one who has been privileged to see a large mass-production organisation working at full pressure.

In order to achieve the scheduled output of finished products, a thousand parts may be needed at a hundred different stages of manufacture. A shortage at any point will hold up the entire factory, a surplus will clog the flow and have repercussions in a variety of ways. Co-ordination, here, requires the provision of means whereby the right parts in the right quantities are made available at the right time in the right places so as to ensure that the right quantity of finished products is achieved. This, though, is a clear-cut and easily assimilated example of co-ordination. It exists— or should exist—too, in a multitude of less easily noticed places.

Every manager has, by definition, the responsibility for directing the activities of others. Directing them is one thing; directing them in accordance with pre-arranged policy is another, but neither will achieve the desired result unless they be so directed that the purpose of direction is accomplished in accordance with an over-riding schedule itself linked to all departments.

It would be useless for the personnel manager to direct one subordinate to interview new staff and another to train them when recruited if, when trained, there were no vacancies for them. This, too, is a simple example but it will serve to illustrate not only the need for co-ordination within each department but also between all departments. The principle of co-ordination cannot, therefore, be omitted.

I come now to the principle of control and I hasten to define this use of the word ; it is one with several meanings. In this sense, control does not mean command or restraint ; it means, in the words of the dictionary, a standard for checking inferences deduced from experiment. This is a less familiar meaning but one often met in management literature. Cost control, for example, does not mean that the cost accountant can make costs whatever he wants them to be. It means that he provides bases against which costs can be checked and compared and means for determining the origins of variations.

Controls of this nature, then, are very important to management. It can never be taken for granted that the optimum is being achieved, however satisfactory everything appears to be. There must always be some basis—control—against which can be compared actual performance. Whether that control be a theoretical ideal or a considered opinion of the best practically attainable matters little. What does matter is that there shall be some such standard of comparison.

Carried to its logical extreme, the principle of control finds expression in budgetary control, a system whereby budgets of expenditure, in the most intricate detail, are laid down in advance ; against these are compared actual expenditures, each responsible person being required to answer to higher management for any departure from the budget.

Even though this method of control is confined to comparatively few firms, it is, nevertheless, impossible for any firm to continue in business for very long unless the basic principle of control be appropriately observed.

Attention has been drawn several times to the importance of realising the dynamic nature of management. The need for development has been stressed and this is a need not only of the technical aspect of industry but also of its managerial aspect. Thus we come to the principle of experiment.

Any firm which sets up, however carefully, an organisation structure suitable to its needs at the time would, before long, find itself in difficulties if it regarded that structure as static. Business conditions change, new methods are introduced, new men are appointed to high office. In these and a hundred other ways is the original structure likely to become divorced from reality.

Add to this that the whole science of management is developing and that new thought is constantly being brought to bear and it will become clear that constant development in management techniques is essential. That development can only come as a result of experiment.

The principle of experiment, therefore, though possibly less obvious, is yet an essential one.

Experiment, though, is not a great deal of use, unless, in total, the lessons of experiment can be learned. To try four or five ways of solving a management problem before finding a workable solution may be satisfactory in one sense but it is of little lasting value unless reasons are clearly attributed to the failure of the abandoned experiments. If an attempt to solve a management problem fails, it must fail for a reason ; therein lies a lesson to be learned. The principle of experiment, therefore, demands more than that experiment must find a place in management ; it demands that those experiments shall be so conducted that the reasons for success or failure can be analysed, classified and used as lessons in subsequent experiments. In short, these experiments must be conducted on scientific lines.

The last principle I am going to discuss is that of elasticity, an obvious need for any competent management. Only if the future could be foreseen with absolute certainty would there be an argument for ignoring this principle.

No management, however, with human limits to its prescience can conceivably afford to set up a structure so unyielding and inflexible that it cannot be influenced by changing fortunes and developing circumstances.

This is not to say that any organisation structure should be so fluid as to lose all cohesion ; it is to say, though, that abstract provision to meet possible changes must be inherent in any structure of management if that management is not to become as extinct, in course of time, as now are the fauna of palæolithic days. The ways of these animals, it will be remembered, were so inelastic that they could not be changed to meet the conditions of a changing world.

I do not want it to be assumed that my list of principles is exhaustive. It isn't. In a science like management, a science developing from an art, he would be rash who would claim to give an exhaustive list of principles. I can only say that I have mentioned those which I believe to be of the very essence of management. Others, of their wisdom, may claim to have crystallised other principles; others, yet again, may break down the principles I have given into still smaller constituent parts; that this can be done is obvious. This book, however, does not presume to be a learned analytical treatise on management theory. Its aim is to help those who have management thrust upon them. For these, I believe that the principles given will suffice as a basis on which to develop their own management thought.

CHAPTER XX

The Practice of Management

Here, at the beginning of the last chapter, it is appropriate to look back and consider in perspective all the subjects that have been discussed. Ranging from a brief survey of the evolution of management to an outline of its principles, the field has been wide but, even so, there is still need for this further chapter designed to translate the inert pages of the book into living, active management.

It would be quite possible, I imagine, for a man to read innumerable books about automobile engineering, for him to take a correspondence course in driving a car, for him to have explained to him by experts the whole of the technique of driving a car and yet, after all this, for him to career madly into the first obstacle in his path when once he was at the wheel. He might, too, be quite unable to isolate and correct an electrical fault or diagnose an unusual note in the engine. All this is to illustrate that there is a wide gulf between knowing the theory of a subject and putting that theory into practice.

The reader should, by now, be reasonably well versed in the theory of management and in the theoretical knowledge of how management is practised. If he has been wise, he will also have related his studies to what he has observed in the course of his job, criticising and complimenting—to himself, of course—all those responsible for carrying out the day-to-day practice of management. It remains, then, to draw attention only to those less obvious ingredients which must be infused into management to give it life. Some will have already found a reference in earlier pages; they are the most important ones and will bear repetition. Others will be new to the reader but all will, on examination, prove to be based on mere common sense.

Even without this chapter, the embryo manager could use what he has already learned. He would, though, have a hard road and make many mistakes before his experience caught up with his theoretical knowledge. By digesting what follows, many of those mistakes can be obviated and the consequences of the remainder can be minimised.

Probably one of the most common causes of inefficient management lies in lack of attention to the organisation structure itself. The organisation structure, as its name implies, is the very framework within which management works. If the framework be faulty, it is little wonder that the management is unequal to its task.

A good organisation structure is one in which each individual has a clear-cut idea of his own responsibilities and is given adequate authority to achieve the required results. Further, those responsibilities must be so related to the functional scheme that no overlapping occurs. There must, too, be first-class liaison between the functional departments at all relevant levels and between the managing director and each of his functional chiefs.

There must be provision for an orderly and well-understood flow of instructions downwards and information upwards. As far as possible this should accord to a standard pattern and all newcomers should be initiated into the system at an early stage in their career.

A good organisation structure, too, calls for forethought to avoid disruption in the event of sickness, accidents and the unexpected generally. This, in turn, requires that each person shall be understudied by someone able, in emergency, to take up the reins and carry on for the time being.

Above all, a good organisation structure demands a loyal and co-operative team of specialists all devoting the whole of their respective abilities to the advancement of the firm's policies. This can be achieved only by high qualities of leadership on the part of the managing director, coupled with an ability to pick the right man for each job and support him to the full.

My next topic is the use of charts as an aid to management

and I must stress that charts can never be a substitute for management. They are an aid, no more.

The purpose of a chart is to illustrate graphically facts which are relevant to the conduct of a business or department. There is, from a management point of view, nothing a chart can show which cannot be shown by figures, but, and this is the important factor, charts, in certain circumstances, can indicate comparisons and trends in such a way that they and their importance can be perceived at a glance.

The practice of management, then, employs charts at top level and at departmental level for a variety of purposes dependent in detail on the individual circumstances peculiar to individual businesses.

In some instances a simple sales chart will suffice; in others production control, sales forecasting, cost analyses, stock turnover and the like may all involve the aid of charts. Remember, though, a wall full of coloured charts is not necessarily an indication of an efficient office.

At high-level management, charts will have a particular value to the members of the Board, who may be out of touch with the day-to-day affairs between Board meetings. It is essential that the Board shall be fully informed of the precise state of the company before any steps are taken to define future policy. To do so in the absence of full and up-to-date knowledge would be to emulate the navigator trying to plot a course without knowing his starting point. Charts provide this basic knowledge.

With their aid, the directors can see how effective has been the existing policy, where it has proved weak or inadequate to meet changing circumstances and what steps must be taken to improve matters in the future.

Reference to the Board and to policy draws attention to another often-found shortcoming in management practice. This is the failure to distinguish between the laying down of policy and its execution. This, perhaps, can be made more clear by developing the navigation analogy.

The Board represents the owners of a ship. They decide how it shall be constructed, what it shall carry, where it shall load and unload, and what freight charges will be sufficient to defray all the innumerable expenses incurred and, at the same time, show a profit. There, their job ends. They do not presume to teach the master how to sail his ship ; they leave full authority in his hands. He is free to give what instructions he deems necessary and to take any desirable action provided only that he gives effect to the decision of his owners.

A managing director is in the position of master of the ship. He has a hand in deciding all the matters already listed and, when decided and agreed, he goes away to carry them out in his own way, knowing that he will have to answer for any faults or mistakes that may occur but freed from any necessity to get detailed instructions from the owners.

The executives of the company are comparable to the ship's officers, each a specialist, in one subject—navigation, marine engineering, victualling and so on in the case of a ship ; selling, development, personnel relations, production and accounting in the case of a business.

Now one thing the master of a ship does not do is spend his time interfering in the work of his officers. He treats them as what they are, specialists, loyal to himself, who know their jobs inside out and can be relied on to do them to the best of their ability. He tells them what is required of them and leaves them to do their own specialised work, he, himself, acting as co-ordinator and final arbiter at need.

Finally in this analogy, the crew is the parallel of the labour force of a factory. Each member of the crew knows whence his own instructions come and to whom he is responsible.

In this way the ship is kept happy, the officers are unhampered, the master is left free to deal with the means of carrying out the owners' requirements and the owners are left to stand or fall by the wisdom of their own decisions, which is all very proper.

Converting this to industrial terms, it is pertinent to wonder how many firms really operate on the same lines.

Probably not very many, though this may be due to the fact that directors are frequently department managers in another capacity and it is easy to see that life at sea might be rather more complicated if the owners and the ship's officers were the same people.

Even so, this is no valid argument against likening a business to a ship. All it means is that the directors, where they do have a dual function, must learn to keep that fact constantly before them and that the managing director, in all his dealings with them, must not confuse the issue by inappropriate discussions and instructions. He, too, must see them in their dual capacities and deal with them accordingly.

Given this reorientation of thought, many of the difficulties of management will be seen in their proper perspective. To appreciate this, think of the number of occasions in your own experience when a director has used his directorial authority in order to over-rule a colleague in a departmental matter. They are legion and, in every case, an affront to the practice of good management.

This, unfortunately, is not the only way in which failure to think clearly and functionally gives rise to troubles and difficulties which are laid usually to the blame of any cause but the right one. I refer to the failure of so many managers to delegate responsibility.

In order to be worth his place in the higher management hierarchy, a manager must have worked his way there by way of a number of junior posts. He may have started as office junior, had charge of a few clerks, understudied an office manager, taken control of a small office and had training in a big department before ultimately becoming a functional executive. In all those posts he will have had certain jobs to do and, by inference, he will have learned to do them well. Being human, he may have come to accept, as part of his thought-process, the adage that says " if you want a thing done well, do it yourself ".

I'm not concerned here to dispute the truth of that adage in any sphere of life, but I am concerned to point out that it just won't work in management. It may be true, but it can't be carried out.

No man with high management responsibility can afford the time to bother his head with the details of all the jobs being done by his subordinates. A managing director can't balance the post-book every night ; a chief accountant can't check every ledger posting individually. If any manager attempts to delve into any such detail, he is at once neglecting his main job which is to manage. It follows that however much he wants to keep his finger in other people's pies, he can only do so by neglecting his own job. This, I suggest, is true, however able the man may be.

The right time to think about delegating responsibilities, then, is when the first step is taken up the managerial ladder ; thereafter it should be a constant consideration at all times, but particularly as further upward steps are taken.

When the office boy is first given promotion with control over, perhaps, the new office boy, his thoughts should turn immediately to a careful analysis of his old job. How many of my old duties, he must ask himself, can I teach to the newcomer ? What checks can I devise to assure myself from time to time that he is carrying out those duties satis-factorily. Some thought on these lines will soon indicate where responsibility can be delegated to the junior while retaining to the upgraded employee an adequate measure of supervision. His new job will thus comprise his new respon-sibilities plus supervision only over the duties he used to perform.

So with the man newly put in charge of a department after several years at a lower level. His first thought must be to shed himself of his old duties by delegating responsibility for them but, it must be remembered, he is not shedding responsibility, he is delegating it. He is still responsible for the results of his subordinates' work, he must still answer for it but, if he's to carry out his new duties, he must relieve himself of his old ones. Instead of doing the jobs of his subordinates he must devise means of seeing that they are done—a shorter but no less responsible task.

If this doctrine of delegation be properly learned, the manager will eventually take over the managing director's office unhampered by hosts of odd jobs that he has collected to himself on the way up. He will be trained in delegating responsibility to those whom the company pays to take it. He will realise that his specialist executives are, in fact, far better able than he is to deal with specialist functions. Realising this, he will not interfere in the way they do their jobs.

He will tell them what policy demands that they shall do and he will leave them to do it in their own ways. He will co-ordinate their efforts because, as managing director, co-ordination is his task. He will satisfy himself that they are working in accordance with his clear instructions and, when the results of their work are to hand, he will reserve to himself the right to accept or reject the advice he receives.

I have set this out, for clarity's sake, as a logical and isolated sequence of events. In day-to-day business, however, the issue of instructions, checks on performance, consultation and assessment of results are all going on practically simultaneously. This, though, does not absolve the managing director from his obligation to free himself from detail so that he can devote his whole time to managing. He, of all executives, has a job of almost pure management, unmixed, as in the case of his executives, with technical pursuits.

Reference was made just now to the means whereby the managing director can satisfy himself that his instructions are being carried out without, personally, involving himself in the detailed execution of those instructions. The need for such means is not confined, of course, to a managing director, it also applies to all managers who have subordinates responsible to them.

The most satisfactory means to this end is the issue of standing instructions calling for certain reports at regular intervals from all subordinate departments or sections. Naturally, the substance and content of these reports must depend on individual circumstances but a great deal of careful thought must go to the compilation of their framework.

Broadly, the reports should consist of statistical representation and the information should be reduced to an absolute minimum consistent with presenting a true picture of results achieved and trends indicated. With them the managing director or department head should be well able to follow the progress being made by his subordinates.

In the case of the managing director, who, of course, has over-riding responsibilities, good management practice dictates that he should implement the report system by more personal contact with his functional executives. He must not, though, interfere in the details of their departmental work.

There are various ways of achieving this personal contact, one of the most usual being the setting up of a management committee consisting of the managing director in the chair and his five or six functional executives with power to co-opt others at need.

This committee can meet monthly or more frequently if required and has an advisory function only. It will fail if the managing director uses it as a means of shifting the responsibility that is rightly his.

The committee can discuss policy in terms of its impact on the various functions, conflicting functional points of view can be integrated, shortcomings in the organisation structure can be traced to their fundamental causes ; in short, the managing director, and through him, the Board, can have the advantage of all the expert advice available. Similarly, the functional executives are enabled to secure wider horizons and become less isolated than would be the case if there were no organised means of discussing problems with their colleagues. A wise managing director will set up a management committee and a wise Board will not ignore its recommendations on future policy.

Effective though a management committee and regular departmental reports can be, management cannot be practised efficiently with these alone. There must, in addition, be a regular and unscheduled flow of information vertically and horizontally through the organisation. Channels for this must be provided and certain rules laid down to ensure that no individual is called upon to deal with matters which are the responsibility of someone senior or junior to him.

Information between departments and the Board must, for instance, be channelled through the managing director; in other cases, information is passed horizontally from one functional executive to another. This, however, could lead to delay if, for example, a foreman were seeking information from a welfare officer. He would, strictly, be obliged to pass the request to his supervisor, thence to the works manager who, in turn, would have to pass it to the personnel manager who would himself have to procure the answer from the welfare officer and transmit it back through the same channels.

To avoid this, the strict interpretation of functional procedure is relaxed and additional lines of contact are set up at various horizontal levels to permit of cross-references on matters of everyday occurrence.

Good management practice cannot be achieved without the realisation of the social responsibilities of management. In this sense, management does not regard the organisation solely as a collection of men and machinery devoted to making money. It recognises that responsibility is owed to its workers who are entitled, at least, to a fair day's pay for a fair day's work; to its shareholders who are entitled to a fair share of the profits in return for the investment of their capital; to its suppliers who are entitled to fair dealing and consideration; and to its customers who are entitled to fair prices and the best possible service. All these factors must find a place when policy is being considered.

Before concluding, I cannot omit mention of a most important personal attribute of management practice.

To be a good manager requires more than a study of management and more than practical experience of management. It requires, too, a distinctive personal attitude.

This attitude, or quality, must have something of leadership in it. The good manager must not only be a good manager, he must be seen to be a good manager and must be able to inspire others to be good managers too. He must command loyalty and respect combined with a faith in his judgement. Only thus can he build and maintain a smooth working team of subordinates. If his actions be suspect, others will tend to supplant his decisions with decisions of their own, jealousies will arise and the team spirit will vanish.

In order to maintain his position, what is known as managerial dignity must be preserved. This, however, must not be confused, or be capable of being confused, with stand-offishness or snobbery.

Managerial dignity, to the onlooker, is that quality which makes a manager rather a mysterious and exalted person ; it does not make him a snob.

By virtue of his position, a manager may be called upon to compliment or reprimand a subordinate at any time or to give instructions involving additional work while the purpose of these instructions may be obscure to their recipient. In all these cases, the manager will only be competent if he has preserved to himself something of an air of dignity, character-ised by a private office and by an aptitude for achieving friendship without familiarity among his subordinates.

A manager who has preserved managerial dignity and is regarded with respect and something akin to awe can award compliments and reprimands with infinitely greater effect than the manager who is on familiar terms with everyone. Further, his instructions are not subject to suspicion and question.

Managerial dignity may be difficult for some to achieve and its balance is fine between over-familiarity and pompous aloofness. Nevertheless, it plays an important part in management practice.

Right at the beginning of this book, I said that to be a good manager requires considerable study and an aptitude for the work, but that there's no magic in management ; there isn't, is there ?

INDEX